C000183822

Culture Wars And Moral Panic

The Story of Alcohol and Society

—

Paul Chase

To Jo

'Best'

Published in Great Britain in 2014 by CPL Publishing

Copyright © 2014 Paul Chase

ISBN No. 978-1-906643-31-7
All rights reserved

CPL Publications
Egerton House
Tower Road
Birkenhead
CH41 1FN
United Kingdom

Contents

Acknowledgements

—

There have been numerous histories of Temperance and of Prohibition that have set out the events and turning points in this area of social history; and there have been previous sociological and political analyses that have sought to characterise public and policy reactions to alcohol in various ways.

In attempting to put my own interpretation on both historical and contemporary events, I have been inspired and informed by the writings of some excellent journalists, notably Phil Mellows and beer writer Pete Brown. Phil's writings on the politics of drinking are shrewd, acerbic and witty; Pete Brown's blogs are what first alerted me to the possibility of deconstructing the arguments of medical temperance by challenging its misuse of statistics. The excellent work of Nigel Hawkes in this regard has also been inspiring, and his website Straight Statistics is both informative and illuminating.

Academics who have contributed to my understanding and analysis by their writings and research include Americans Stanton Peele and Joseph R. Gusfield, whose pioneering works on addiction and the social construction of alcohol problems, respectively, remain classics that have stood the test of time. I am indebted also to Frank Furedi, Professor of Sociology at the University of Kent, Canterbury, UK, whom I have never met, but whose writings have provided me with numerous philosophical and sociological insights over many years.

Thanks are also due to Daniel Davies, my long-time friend and business partner at CPL Training, whose generous offer to finance the publication of this book is greatly appreciated. Thanks also to Mike Haslam for his close textual attention.

We all stand on the shoulders of others when we attempt any literary or research project. I have cited the scholarship and authorship of those named above, and many others in the body of the text. However, any mistakes or omissions remain entirely my own, and I take responsibility for the ideas, beliefs, opinions and conclusions that I express in this book.

Paul Chase, Wirral, May 2014

Introduction

—

WHY HAVE I WRITTEN THIS BOOK?

I have spent most of my adult life working in the licensed retail sector, directly or indirectly. From my early years as a student working behind the bar, to operating and holding licences on late-night licensed premises on Merseyside; for over 20 years I worked in licensed premises. And overlapping with this direct experience, for a further 20 years, and currently, as a Director of CPL Training, engaged in training and preparing people who are just starting out in the sector.

I did my growing-up in this industry. During the course of my career I have been exposed to extraordinary people, experiences and challenges that I doubt would have been available to me in any other walk of life. It distresses me to see the way in which the industry is today pilloried by those who present a grotesque distortion of reality that I just don't recognise.

I am motivated not just by a desire to understand the past, but to use that historical understanding as a means to make sense of the current moral panic over alcohol.

WHAT IS THE SCOPE OF THIS BOOK?

The book is divided into three parts and is designed to be read sequentially and understood as a whole. Nevertheless, each part of the book can be read separately, and I hope will make sense as an essay in its own right. I present an historical discourse together with an analysis that is informed by, and framed within sociological and political theory.

WHO IS IT AIMED AT?

Naturally I would want this book to be read by as wide an audience as possible. My target audiences are (in no particular order) the political establishment, agents of influence in the media and my peers in the licensed retail sector. My intent is to reignite what Joseph R. Gusfield would call a 'contest of meanings' and to challenge the cultural ownership of the alcohol issue by clerics and medics.

WHITHER 'CULTURE WAR' AND 'MORAL PANIC'?

A recurrent theme of this book is that political conflict over alcohol mediates wider religious, political and cultural anxieties; that opposition to alcohol, and to the people engaged in making and selling it, has historically taken the form of a series of symbolic crusades in which the actors themselves are often unwitting agents of a cultural determinism that they perceive as through a glass, but darkly. These symbolic crusades represent 'culture wars' in the sense that social groups with different religious and cultural values have used alcohol issues as a means of contesting political and cultural hegemony.

'Moral panic' is a term which is itself academically controversial and subject to a number of different definitions. The sense in which I use the term in this book, and feel justified in describing past and current controversies surrounding alcohol as 'moral panics', is best understood if we consider the definition of moral panic given by the originator of the term, sociologist Stanley Cohen:

"Societies appear to be subject, every now and then, to periods of moral panic. A condition, episode, person or groups of persons emerges to become defined as a threat to societal values and interests; its nature is presented in a stylized and stereotypical fashion by the mass media; the moral barricades are manned by editors, bishops, politicians and other right-thinking people; socially accredited experts pronounce their diagnoses and solutions; ways of coping are evolved (or more often) resorted to; the condition then disappears, submerges, or deteriorates and becomes more visible." *(Cohen 1972 p.9)*

Moral panics can therefore be understood as both official and unofficial reactions to certain social phenomenon that are entirely disproportionate to the actual level of threat posed. It is my contention that the current heightened alarm over the effects of alcohol consumption exemplifies just such a moral panic. Furthermore, that its antecedents display many commonalities with the current situation. This book seeks to explore how and why that is, and to locate the various episodes of moral panic in relation to alcohol within longer term processes of moral regulation.

THE BOOK IS DIVIDED INTO THREE PARTS:

PART 1: THE HISTORY OF ALCOHOL AS A SOCIAL PROBLEM

Chapter 1: American Temperance and Prohibition
In this chapter I trace and analyse the main events and turning points in the 'Wets vs. Dries' political conflicts of the 19th and early 20th centuries that eventually led to the prohibition of alcohol in the United States in 1920.

Chapter 2: UK Temperance and Licensing
In this chapter I trace and analyse the history of the Temperance movement in the UK that culminated in a failed attempt by the Liberal Government of Henry Campbell-Bannerman and his Chancellor Herbert Asquith to nationalise the pub industry in 1908, and at the partial nationalisation that took place at the outset of WWI.

Chapter 3: Temperance Worldwide
In this chapter I examine some of the commonalities between UK and US Temperance and temperance movements in other countries, in terms of the influence of organised religion on the development of temperance sentiment.

PART 2: FROM CLERICS TO MEDICS

Chapter 1: Establishing Cultural Authority
In this chapter I discuss the process by means of which a social phenomenon becomes a social issue. I examine the role of moral entrepreneurs in establishing the conceptual and cultural frame of reference through which politicians, and the wider public, are invited to understand 'the issues'. I also examine how cultural ownership of the 'alcohol problem' has passed from clerics to medics;

Chapter 2: The Disease Theory of Alcoholism and Public Health Perspectives
In this chapter I explain the early development of mainstream alcohol science in the United States. I compare and contrast historical and contemporary public health approaches to dealing with alcohol and provide a critical historical discourse analysis of the new public health movement.

Chapter 3: The Sociological Challenge to Public Health Orthodoxy

In this chapter I discuss how a social constructionist approach to understanding alcohol use can provide the means by which to challenge the cultural hegemony of medical temperance and its neo-prohibitionist aspiration. I place contemporary alcohol use in the context of historical social ritual and changes to the way in which we divide work and leisure.

PART 3: THE ARCHITECTURE OF A MODERN MORAL PANIC

Chapter 1: The Temperance Beast Awakes!

In this chapter I examine recent social and legal history leading up to the implementation of the Licensing Act 2003. I discuss how the presentation of this reform awoke dormant cultural anxieties about alcohol use and its impacts on society. I present the evidence that the neo-prohibitionist response to licensing reform represents a media-led moral panic of the first order.

Chapter 2: The Neo-prohibitionist Attack on the Alcohol Industry

In this chapter I discuss the intellectual underpinnings of the current neo-prohibitionist attack on the alcohol industry. I examine the roots of the view that alcohol is 'no ordinary product' by reference to French research conducted during WWII. I discuss how historical moral temperance and modern medical temperance became aligned in the Alcohol Health Alliance, and reasserted their cultural ownership of the alcohol issue.

Chapter 3: What is to be done? Towards a Contest of Meanings

In this chapter I ask what can a fractious alcohol industry do to counter the relentless attacks of the neo-prohibitionists? I examine the prospects for the alcohol industry of mounting a successful contest of meanings, in the context of a risk-averse society where the societal values of 'health and safety' and preventative public health increasingly infantilises adult decision-making.

Part 1

The History of Alcohol as a Social Problem

—

Temperance Ladies

Chapter 1:

American Temperance and Prohibition

—

In this chapter I trace the main events and turning points in the 'Wets vs. Dries' political conflicts of the 19th and early 20th centuries that eventually led to the prohibition of alcohol in the United States in 1920.

I examine some of the underlying religious and cultural anxieties that animated a political conflict that spanned over 100 years, and which has left a lasting legacy in American politics. It is a recurrent theme of this book that moral panics about alcohol occur in particular kinds of society, and that they are frequent not exceptional. I also argue that such events should not simply be taken at face-value, but analysed to discover the architecture of their symbolism, in order to uncover an objective reality that lies beyond subjective perceptions.

In the course of this analysis I will also look at a number of organisations and prominent individuals, many of them larger-than-life characters, and the role they played as actors in the culture war and moral panic that led to Prohibition and its eventual repeal.

THE IDEA OF AMERICA

US President Richard Nixon made an historic visit to China in 1972, widely credited as a foreign policy triumph that opened up China to the world. Before he went Nixon's Secretary of State Henry Kissinger told him about Chinese Premier Chou en Lai's obsession with French history; so Nixon, who fancied himself as something of an intellectual, asked Chou what the most significant long-term effects of the French Revolution had been on western civilisation. Chou en Lai famously replied: "It's too early to tell." If Nixon hoped to convince Chou that the French Revolution was a failed socialist experiment that ended in the collapse of the Paris Commune, whereas the American Revolution, which started 13 years earlier, had endured, he was to be disappointed. When Chou gave his enigmatic response it is doubtful that the shrewd old despot was being humorous, much less predicting that either America or Nixon wouldn't have a long-term; more likely that his concept of what constituted the long-term was very Chinese, and therefore very long-term indeed.

What is beyond doubt, however, is that the ideas of *liberté, egalité et fraternité* were not just a French *cri de coeur*, but a cry that rang out around the world. Without the philosophical ideas of the European Enlightenment neither the American Revolutionary War of Independence nor the French Revolution would have been possible. The revolutions they inspired arose out of the material and political conditions of an American people who wanted to cast off colonialism, and a French people whose needs were not being met by an *ancien régime* whose time had passed.

The American Revolution challenged the idea that the nation-state was just tribalism writ large. It posited the notion that it was possible to forge a nation on the basis of belief in a political idea. That idea was 'citizenship' and it was a very big idea indeed.

It is, of course, far too simplistic to view America as a melting-pot society into whose soup contributing nationalisms, tribalisms, religious and cultural differences were all subsumed by a liberal sprinkling of citizenship, and mediated by a written constitution. The poem inscribed on the base of the Statue of Liberty reads "Give me your tired, your poor, your huddled masses yearning to breathe free, the wretched refuse of your teeming shore". But early emigrants to America, although keen to escape the stifling restrictions and religious persecution of the Old World, nevertheless brought their cultures, values, religions, drinking habits and rituals with them to the New World. Each group struggled to make its mark and to establish its own traditions as the benchmark and norm to which future generations of immigrants should adhere.

COMING TO AMERICA

The American colonial period began on the 14th May, 1607 with the landing of British colonists on what was later called Jamestown Island, Virginia. It ended on the 4th July, 1776 with the American Declaration of Independence from the English Crown.

The early American colonies were ethnically and culturally homogeneous. In these tight-knit communities the family and local community was the mediator of drinking patterns, and drinking problems do not appear to have loomed large, despite rumblings of discontent from the courts and the clergy. This was true despite the fact that alcohol consumption per head was several times its current level in the United States. As reported by researchers (*Zinberg and Fraser 1979*) drunkenness rates were lower, despite higher levels of consumption.

The concept of alcoholism, as we understand it today, did not exist. Alcohol was seen generally as a benign substance and its use socially positive. Drinking to get drunk was seen as a personal choice, not as a disease. The idea of alcoholism as an uncontrollable disease was introduced much later in the colonial period by the physician Dr Benjamin Rush. In 1785 he published his 'Inquiry into the Effects of Ardent Spirits upon the Human Body and Mind, and its Influence upon the Happiness of Society'. Then, in 1808 Dr. Billy J. Clark formed the first recorded total abstinence society in New York.

TOBACCO, ALCOHOL AND SLAVERY

Jamestown, Virginia was the first permanent English settlement in North America. It was on the verge of economic collapse when farmer John Rolfe planted its first tobacco crop in 1612. That crop fetched a good price a year later back in London, generating new interest and financial investment for the Virginia colony. Soon Virginia's entire existence revolved around growing tobacco for export. By 1618, the Virginians produced 20,000 pounds of tobacco a year. In 1619 they resorted to slavery to fill the expanding need for labour to harvest the tobacco crops. Slavery and tobacco would dominate the Virginia economy for the next 240 years.

Meanwhile, in Colonial New England the economy was dominated not by a smoking product, but by the production and sale of an intoxicating drink – rum.

THE RUM ECONOMY

By the 1650s New Englanders had opened dozens of distilleries, importing molasses from the West Indies for processing into strong rum. As early as 1661 the General Court of Massachusetts ruled that excess rum production in the colony was damaging society. In 1686, a prominent Massachusetts preacher, with the improbable name of Increase Mather, lamented that "a kind of drink called rum has been common among us. They that are poor, and wicked too, can for a penny or tuppence make themselves drunk." But neither lawyers nor preachers could dent the popularity of rum. Rum production continued to rise; by 1770, New England had over a 140 rum distilleries. That same year, the 1.7 million people who populated the thirteen colonies drank 7.5 million gallons of rum; that's 4.4 gallons for every person – man, woman and child - then living in America.

Such heavy demand for rum made it the mainstay of the colonial New England economy. By the eve of the American Revolution, rum accounted for more than 80% of the region's exports. The rum trade drew New England merchants into the growing international marketplace that would soon give birth to modern capitalism. New England's traders imported molasses from the West Indies, distilled it into strong rum, and then exported it — especially to Africa where it could be exchanged for valuable cargoes of slaves. The slaves could then be sold again, at great profit, to the tobacco and cotton farmers of the American South or to the sugar planters of the West Indies who would send back molasses, which would then be distilled into rum to start the cycle anew.

This was the infamous 'triangular trade' in rum, slaves, and molasses and it turned Newport, Rhode Island, into the most important slave port in North America; by 1776, Rhode Islanders controlled nearly 90% of the American slave trade.

Thus, the rise of the American economy, and its development into the greatest generator of wealth in human history began with the 17th century trade in tobacco, alcohol and slaves.

18TH CENTURY AMERICA

18th century America continued to be a rural society. Despite the development of big plantations in the south, new settlers were attracted by the opportunity to own and work the land in small farms where the whole family was employed in subsistence farming. There was no sharp delineation between work and leisure, and alcohol use was a social ritual woven into the fabric of everyday life. Whether it was raising a barn, building a church, haggling over the price of provisions in the local store – none of these things happened without the intoxicating lubrication of a jug of rum.

19TH CENTURY AMERICA

Although the organised movement for Prohibition didn't take off until after the end of the American Civil War in 1865, the spread of support for temperance (moderate use of alcohol) and for abstinence began earlier. In early 19th century America support for this was primarily amongst rural and small-town Protestant, middle-class, white Americans. The fact that support for temperance and abstinence grew at a time when new waves of immigrants were coming to America was no coincidence. Immigrants from Ireland and Germany, who settled in the larger towns and cities, and who were mostly Catholic, impecunious and working class, brought with them traditions of hard drinking. For the established American Protestant middle class, asserting the norms of temperance and abstinence was a way of saying to the newcomers 'my house, my rules'.

It is perhaps no surprise, therefore, that these early American 'culture wars' took on a symbolic form. The struggle over the 'alcohol question' is but one example of a symbolic crusade in which the victory of 'dries' over 'wets' would come to symbolise the cultural hegemony of one religious and cultural group over another.

And race, which is to America what social class is to Britain, also played its part. Fears of what 'drunken negroes' might do began to be woven into popular social discourse about alcohol.

The essential point is that it was not the use, or even the excessive use of alcohol that caused a reactionary demand for temperance and abstinence. Cultural competition, and its attendant anxieties, set that dialectic in motion.

THE FIRST WAVE: EARLY TEMPERANCE ORGANISATIONS

Organisations that opposed alcohol consumption began before the American Civil War that raged between 1861 and 1865. The American Temperance Society was formed in Boston, Massachusetts in 1826 and over a five-year period developed a membership in excess of 170,000. The Society for the Suppression of Intemperance and the Society for the Promotion of Temperance were formed shortly afterwards. An offshoot, The Sons of Temperance, claimed a membership of some 200,000 people and, inevitably, was joined by The Daughters of Temperance in the 1840s.

This emphasis on protecting the young from the alleged evils of the demon drink was augmented by the creation of The Order of the Sons of Temperance Friendly Society. This organisation proffered "Unsurpassed Sick & Assurance Benefits for Men, Women & Children" and exhorted citizens to "Safeguard the Young by Enrolling Them as Cadets of Temperance".

These early temperance organisations began by calling for moderate alcohol use – true temperance – what today we would call 'responsible drinking', but that soon became a call for voluntary abstinence or what was later called 'teetotalism'. When the power of persuasion failed to deliver the desired number of volunteers, the movement and its organisations converted to coercive reform and called for outright legal prohibition of the production, sale and transportation of beverage alcohol.

Prohibition Campaign Poster

It is perhaps a sobering thought that today, in the theocratic government of Iran, there is a Ministry for the Suppression of Vice and the Promotion of Virtue. Back in 19th century America, where separation of Church and State was written into the Constitution, we see the same sentiment expressed, albeit thinly disguised, whereby 'intemperance' and 'temperance' are substitute words for 'vice' and 'virtue'.

RELIGIOUS AND CULTURAL SYMBOLISM

These early temperance organisations reflected the religious values of ascetic forms of Protestantism. Cultural anxieties were engendered by waves of immigrants from European countries, where Lutheran or Catholic religious traditions emphasised confessionary rituals (commit sin, feel guilty, confess and repent). These anxieties animated activists from Calvinist-inspired, individualistic religious traditions that emphasised personal self-control and self-denial. Campaigning for abstinence and prohibition therefore symbolised the desire of established Protestant, 'nativist' Americans to enshrine a system of moral regulation in law, using cultural ownership of a socially constructed 'alcohol problem' to emphasise their cultural hegemony.

The early temperance movement had some success. In the 1840s 13 states banned the production and sale of intoxicating liquors. Licensed saloons were closed down and social drinking driven underground into unlicensed 'drinking dens'. Many of these unlicensed establishments exploited a loophole in the law which permitted complementary alcoholic drinks to be served at exhibitions of natural wonders. Such places stretched the definition of 'natural wonder' to breaking point and were often ironically referred to as 'blind tiger' or 'blind pig' establishments.

Clearly, the ever-more imaginative ways of avoiding these laws, or simply ignoring them, exposed this early experiment with prohibition as a failure, and 12 out of the 13 states repealed their dry laws.

After the *dénouement* of state-wide prohibition America's obsession with the evils of alcohol was replaced with concern over a much greater evil; one that was destined to tear the American nation apart: slavery.

THE SECOND WAVE: POST-CIVIL WAR AMERICAN TEMPERANCE AND PROHIBITION

The American Civil War raged from 1861 to 1865. Although ostensibly the abolition of slavery was the reason for it, the idea that this vicious conflict arose because two opposing camps of white people, each claiming that God was on their side, fought over the emancipation of black people confers on this struggle a sense of nobility it doesn't really deserve. The emancipation of the slaves was the public moral justification for an existential fight over nationhood, money and power.

Would America be a loose confederation of states with a weak centre, in which the rights of the individual state would always trump the rights and powers of the federal authority? Or would it be a unitary state in which the federal authority would achieve supremacy, and from which a strong, politically centralised nation-state would evolve?

At the heart of this was the currency issue, and as we shall see, temperance organisations took a political position on this issue, which they regarded as crucial to the realisation of their aims. From the start there was confusion over money. The early American colonists used English, French and Spanish currency. The original issue of American paper money, by the Massachusetts Bay Colony in 1690, was in the form of 'Colonial Notes'. In 1775 'Continental Currency' was issued by the Continental Congress to finance the Revolutionary War, but this was issued in anticipation of taxes that didn't materialise and was worthless paper money.

The federal monetary system was established in 1792, and the minting of the first Federal American dollar coins in 1793, by the US Mint in Philadelphia, signalled an important change. But individual states were still allowed to print their own bank notes and by 1836, with minimal regulation, some 1,600 state-chartered, private banks were still issuing their own paper money, with over 30,000 varieties of paper quality, note size, colour and design. Counterfeiting was rife. Small town newspaper proprietors were notorious for it. After all, if you published the 'Hicksville Star' once a week, what were you supposed to do with your printing press on the other six days?

This huge variety of money, along with frequent bank failures, led to confusion and circulation problems. Money was not performing its basic function of a reliable means of exchange in which people had confidence, nor was it a store of value.

If the American economy was to expand, a single currency was needed. The pre-requisite for that was a single polity; hence the Civil War. One of the earliest acts of the Department of the Treasury, after the Civil War ended in 1865, was to establish the United States Secret Service with the sole express purpose of eliminating counterfeit money, which was estimated to account for about one third of all money then in circulation. The defeat of the Confederacy settled these issues. It led to the abolition of slavery, the assertion of Federal Government supremacy and the establishment, over 40 years, of a single currency, a Treasury and the Federal Reserve as lender of last resort.

The relevance of all this for temperance and prohibition is that the Women's Christian Temperance Union (WCTU), and other temperance organisations, took a political position on the currency issue. They realised that without a single currency there couldn't be an effective system of federal income tax. Without income tax the federal government would continue to rely on the taxation of tobacco and alcohol as its principal sources of revenue, and whilst that remained the case the achievement of national prohibition would be impossible. Federal income tax was introduced in 1913 and paved the way for national prohibition of beverage alcohol production, transportation and sale in 1920.

The American State was thus able to put in place the political and monetary underpinnings that galvanised the creation of an entrepreneurial and industrial giant, the like of which the world had never seen before.

It also reignited the culture war over alcohol, and helped to spawn the 'second Ku Klux Klan', which became an enthusiastic supporter of prohibition. The second Ku Klux Klan was founded in 1915 by William J. Simmonds and its formation was intended to widen its racist and nationalist appeal. It stood for white supremacy, intense 'nativism' and was also anti-Catholic. These last two characteristics aligned it with temperance campaigners who sought to reassert the values of the original settlers – 'nativist' Americans - and their descendants. In the wake of the Civil War earlier grievances and anxieties had resurfaced. Nativist Americans, who were mostly Protestant religionists, saw themselves as the custodians of American values; their country had undergone the most fearsome upheaval and they felt threatened by Catholicism and feared racial integration and large-scale immigration.

THE PROTESTANT WORK ETHIC AND THE SPIRIT OF CAPITALISM

Whilst the American Civil War can be seen as a necessary pre-condition for the further development of American capitalism, when Max Weber later wrote of the "Protestant Work Ethic and the Spirit of Capitalism" he encapsulated what had become a major rationalising ideology for early and later temperance and abstinence campaigns. After the Civil War the accelerated development of American capitalism, mass manufacturing and urbanisation created huge social dislocation, separated labour from its tools, aggregated capital in a factory system and led, crucially, to a new requirement that work-time and leisure-time should to be separated one from the other. The unfolding of these economic and social dynamics demonstrated a complex relationship between the economic sub-structure and the cultural superstructure. How this dialectic played out, and how it was reflected in the consciousness of individuals led in turn to an interest-group status-conflict of epic proportions.

The development of an industrial capitalism, based on mass manufacturing and the division of labour, led to the rapid migration of country folk into the burgeoning towns and cities of industrial America. These towns and cities were the locus of hard-drinking Irish and German Catholic immigrants who packed the saloons and engaged in licentious behaviour. Such Godless activity had to be opposed; it threatened the work ethic and challenged the moral and cultural mores of the nativist, Protestant rural middle class. And so the battle between Wets and Dries, which threw up organisations and individuals some of whom we may today see as cartoon characters, was nothing less than a fight for the religious, moral and cultural soul of America.

THE WOMEN'S CRUSADE

Pre-eminent amongst the plethora of Temperance organisations that flourished before and after the Civil War was the Women's Christian Temperance Union (WCTU). Its genesis can be traced back to the Ohio

Dr Diocletian Lewis

Women's Crusade that was ignited by a sermon delivered by one Dr Diocletian Lewis, on the night before Christmas Eve, 1873.

Dr Lewis's claim to be a doctor was based on an honorary degree in homeopathic studies, but despite being unlicensed he practised medicine in Buffalo, New York. The subject of his sermon in Hillsboro's Baptist church on this night was entitled: "The Duty of Christian Women in the Cause of Temperance." In the course of this address, which he had delivered many times, he invited the women present to take direct action - to confront and shame the liquor trade by engaging in prayer vigils and hymn-singing in premises that sold liquor.

Picture the scene: the distinguished looking, bearded "Dr Dio"; the shining, eager, upturned faces of the assembled congregation of Christian women, their corseted bodices swelling with messianic fervour; the fiery address of the thundering preacher, and then the call to action! The very next night – Christmas Eve - some 50 women were thereby sufficiently imbued with morally self-righteous vim and vigour to embark on a series of peaceful prayer vigils and hymn-singing in Hillsboro's saloons, rum shops and drug stores. Most of Hillsboro's saloon owners pledged to shut-up shop, or at least to stop selling rum and whiskey. In the New Year the word spread and the matriarchy was well and truly on the march. The campaign rapidly expanded, and thousands of women joined the Women's Crusade, which succeeded in closing saloons in 912 communities in 31 states across America.

The campaign waxed high throughout the first half of 1874, but waned towards the summer months when many of the saloons that had closed quietly re-opened their doors. But the lesson of the Women's Crusade

Frances E. Willard

was that it needed leadership and organisation if it was to be sustained. One person who clearly understood that lesson was a bright 35 year-old professor of aesthetics, who was at that time employed by Chicago's Northwestern University. Her name was Frances E. Willard. Willard's father was a farmer and her mother a school teacher. Her father was also a naturalist and legislator and had moved the family to Oberlin, Ohio, to be part of the ministry there. It was during the family's stay in Wisconsin that they converted from Congregationalists to Methodists; Methodism being a non-conformist Protestant denomination that places great emphasis on social justice and service to humanity.

In the 1860s Willard's father and younger sister Mary both died and her brother became an alcoholic. Willard herself fell in love with a woman who would eventually go on to marry Willard's brother. A Methodist and teetotaller haunted by personal tragedy and thwarted in her love life, Frances Willard was a rebel without a cause. She quickly found one in Temperance.

THE WOMEN'S CHRISTIAN TEMPERANCE UNION (WCTU)

Following the Women's Crusade, the inaugural national convention of the WCTU took place in Cleveland, Ohio in November 1874. It appointed Mrs Annie Turner Wittenmyer as its first National President.

Frances Willard, who had earlier taken part in her first saloon vigil, joined hundreds of like-minded souls at this seminal event. Her exceptional intelligence and high academic standing recommended her to delegates, and she was appointed as the WCTU's Corresponding Secretary. She later went on to draft its Declaration of Principles. These championed protection of the home and the abolition of the liquor traffic as the means to achieve this. Five years later she became the WCTU's leader, a position she held until her death of influenza in September, 1898, aged just 58.

WOMANS HOLY WAR.
Grand Charge on the Enemy's Works.

The WCTU slogan was "For God and Home and Native Land" – later changed to "Every Land". Initially the WCTU hoped that education of the masses and their own good moral example would be sufficient to obtain pledges of total abstinence from alcohol, and later from tobacco and other drugs. Those who 'took the pledge' wore white ribbons as the symbol of their purity, and their approach to reform was summed-up by their slogan "Agitate – Educate – Legislate". But when moral suasion proved insufficient, they turned, like other temperance groups, to coercive reform.

The WCTU was organised in 'chapters' throughout North America and local chapters were known as 'unions'. But the word 'Christian' in its title ensured its membership was largely limited to those of an evangelical Protestant conviction. This meant that very few Catholics, Jews, Moslems, Buddhists or Sikhs were attracted to its ranks, notwithstanding the fact that it became a worldwide movement and that the last three of these were religiously and culturally in favour of abstinence.

The first President of WCTU, Annie Wittenmyer, believed that it should dedicate itself to a single purpose – promoting abstinence from alcohol. She saw this as a moral campaign aiming to persuade those of lower moral standing (principally men) to aspire to the higher moral standing of women. They strongly believed that women were the more 'moral' sex and drinking was seen as a personal moral failure, rather than being caused by the institutions that facilitated access to alcohol. The idea that women were more moral and religious than men and that the home was therefore an important moral and religious sphere was also common in Britain in the late 18th and early 19th centuries. This wing of the WCTU offered what has been referred to as an "assimilative moral invitation" (Joseph R. Gusfield 'Symbolic Crusade'): the way for the immigrant, working class newcomer to join the nativist, middle class Americans – for each of 'them' to become 'one of us' - was to accept the social prescriptions of their supposed moral superiors.

After becoming WCTU President, Willard broadened the range of issues that the organisation championed. At this time women did not have the vote and Willard became a leading suffragist. She extended the WCTU's work to embrace a number of other moral causes, including legislation to protect working girls from the exploitation of men; aiding immigrants arriving at Ellis Island by 'Americanising' them; sabbatarianism and the restriction of frivolous activities. For example, in 1901 the WCTU said that golf should not be allowed on Sundays!

The WCTU was also concerned to combat poverty. But it didn't advocate higher wages, redistribution of income, or socialising the means of production in order to achieve this, but rather abstinence from alcohol was seen as the way forward. One of the reasons why early American capitalists, such as Henry Ford and John D. Rockefeller, felt able enthusiastically to endorse the abstinence and prohibition movement was its belief that the way to combat poverty was to morally reform the consumption patterns of the poor, by eliminating expenditure on alcohol and tobacco, in order to release more money for hearth and home.

The fact that this would deliver to them a more sober, disciplined workforce with a better work-ethic and without challenging their power or control represented a powerful motive for supporting the temperance and prohibition movements. Middle class moral reform and the interests of capitalism were clearly aligned. Henry Ford even rewarded sobriety and temperance with higher wages and company social workers were employed to spread the word and encourage temperance and sobriety.

Many of those who have recounted the life of Frances Willard have portrayed her as a sainted figure; a true Renaissance woman. Her restless energy led her to embrace women's suffrage, the right of workers to organise in trades unions, federal aid to education, free school lunches, the eight-hour working day, boards of health, anti-rape laws, and municipal sanitation – to name just a few.

But whilst she was a radical, and in certain respects a progressive thinker, she was a prisoner of at least some of the prejudices of her day. She had a bitter conflict with African-American journalist Ida B. Wells over her failure to condemn the lynching of black men, and her attitude to the relationship between alcoholic liquor and black criminality. Wells criticised Willard's willingness to drum-up support for Temperance in the South by pandering to the racist myth that white women were in constant danger of rape from black males made lustful by drink.

Quoted in a New York temperance newspaper *The Voice* Willard had commented:

"Alien illiterates rule our cities today; the saloon is their palace, and the toddy stick their sceptre. It is not fair that they should vote, nor is it fair that a plantation Negro, who can neither read nor write, whose ideas are bounded by the fence of his own field and the price of his own mule should be entrusted with the ballot. The colored race multiplies like the locusts of Egypt. The grog-shop is their center of power. The safety of women, of childhood, of the home is menaced in a thousand localities at this moment."

Ida B. Wells

When Wells took this article to England, where Willard was already a popular speaker, and attempted to have it republished, she was prevented from doing so by Lady Henry Somerset, Willard's lover and UK host.

To be fair to Willard, the WCTU had actively recruited black women to its membership, but had never spoken out against lynching in the south. After the exchange with Wells, Willard made her opposition to lynching plain and the WCTU passed a motion opposing it.

So the WCTU contained within its membership socially conservative thinkers who wanted the organisation to focus on temperance and abstinence, as well as progressive thinkers who wanted the alcohol issue to be placed in a broader context of enlightened social reform. But the move from moral suasion to coercive legal reform is what characterised the organisation under Willard's leadership.

THE DEPARTMENT OF SCIENTIFIC TEMPERANCE INSTRUCTION IN SCHOOLS AND COLLEGES

This was the brainchild of one Mary Hanchet-Hunt who eclipsed Frances Willard as the most powerful woman advocate of prohibition. She had been a school teacher when, in the early 1870s, she persuaded her local school board in Massachusetts to establish temperance instruction in its schools. Hunt and a colleague, Julia Coleman, then sought to extend their influence to other school boards in the state. They created lessons on hygiene and physiology and Coleman produced a textbook on the subject entitled "Alcohol and Hygiene."

Mary Hanchet-Hunt

In 1879 Willard invited Hunt to speak at the WCTU's national convention on the subject of "Scientific Temperance Instruction". At the convention Hunt expounded her ideas for inculcating abstinence into school children by the compulsory study of textbooks on 'scientific temperance'. A WCTU standing committee on the subject was then established, which was replaced a year later by a Department of Scientific Temperance Instruction in Schools and Colleges, of which Mary Hunt became the National Superintendent.

This linking of science and moral suasion was typical of the time. The extraordinary sensation caused by the publication, on the 24th November 1859, of Charles Darwin's book 'On the Origin of Species' had made science fashionable. Marxists, for example, attempted to base their ideological appeal on 'scientific socialism'; and claims that personal, political or moral views had scientific validity, that they weren't merely subjective, was seen as *de rigeur*. Progressive thinkers, and others who wished to present themselves as 'modernists', sought to associate their views with science, and in so doing lend a spurious legitimacy to the most tendentious of claims.

Under Hunt's influence WCTU local chapters began exerting pressure on local school boards across the country to introduce compulsory temperance education. This siege strategy produced disappointing results despite the fact that Hunt had, herself, in 1880 spoken at 182 school board meetings. More generally WCTU was encountering push-back from those who were not persuaded by the temperance credo. During the course of the 1880s there were 20 state prohibition referenda, 12 of which were defeated and in the rest enforcement was patchy at best. Hunt reached the obvious conclusion: that this was going to be a long haul and the task to educate the next generation of voters must begin. As she put it, voters "must first be convinced that alcohol and kindred narcotics are by nature outlaws, before they will outlaw them". And so the compulsory Scientific Temperance Instruction Movement was born.

Hunt was convinced that legislation was needed and she encouraged WCTU members to put pressure on state legislators and to promote the candidacy of pro-temperance candidates at election time. The State of Vermont was the first state in which this strategy was trialled. Letter writing campaigns, the endorsement of prominent citizens, petitions, packing meetings with temperance supporters of the proposed Temperance Instruction Bill were all tactics employed for the first time in Vermont. The bill was passed and became law in 1882 *(Norton Mezvinsky, Scientific temperance instruction in schools. History of Education Quarterly, 1961, 7, p.49).*

The campaign moved on to Michigan and Hunt was determined that the laws requiring temperance instruction in schools would be increasingly prescriptive, and that they would be strictly enforced. The whole strategy of support for educating the young in the evils of alcohol was much safer for politicians than actually proscribing the use of alcohol amongst adult voters, so local politicians felt obliged to support the campaign. Compliance with temperance teaching laws was monitored and enforced by local WCTU Superintendents visiting the schools in their locality and woe betide recalcitrant teachers or school boards who were tardy in their attitude to these legally enforced moral strictures!

This was a hugely successful campaign of coercive moral suasion and within 20 years of its start every state in the Union had laws requiring anti-alcohol education. The textbooks approved by Mary Hunt and endorsed by the

WCTU were required to state that "any quantity of alcohol in any form was toxic and when consumed regularly produced inheritable disorders into the third generation." *(John Kobler, Ardent Spirits: The Rise and Fall of Prohibition, 1973 p. 140).*

In fact the textbooks approved by Hunt and the Department of Scientific Temperance Instruction in Schools and Colleges made a mockery of science. They promoted as "scientifically proven fact" that:

- The majority of beer drinkers die from dropsy
- When alcohol passes down the throat it burns off the skin
- It causes the heart to beat many unnecessary times and after the first dose the heart is in danger of giving out, so the drinker has to take drink after drink to keep it going
- It turns blood into water
- Invalids who would otherwise recover would surely die if they were drinkers

(John Kobler, 1973, p. 143)

The approved textbooks seem to have been written with the object of frightening young, impressionable children into believing that even the most moderate use of alcohol would transport them to the top of a slippery slope. As approved textbooks asserted: "To attempt to drink fermented liquors moderately has led to the untold ruin of thousands." *(John S. Billings, The Liquor Problem: A Summary of Investigations Conducted by the Committee of Fifty 1903 pp. 30-34).*

Mary Hunt's assertions were increasingly criticised by leading scientists and educators. Those who criticised were emboldened by the report published by the highly influential Committee of Fifty that was formed in 1893 to study the 'liquor problem'. Eminent sociologists criticised the increasingly exaggerated claims and a sub-committee of the Committee, headed by faculty members from Clark and Harvard Universities, found the Hunt-WCTU approach to alcohol education seriously defective.

The Report surveyed all members of the American Physiological Society, and in addition some 45 physiologists and hygienists from other countries, in an attempt to articulate an authoritative scientific consensus on 'scientific temperance' claims. Although many of these scientists were themselves anti-alcohol, all but one of them refuted the main claims made in the Hunt-WCTU textbooks. The view of the Committee of Fifty was best summed up in this extract:

"As is generally the case when feeling and prejudice run high, the temptation has been irresistible to either manufacture scientific evidence or stretch it over points that it does not cover; to call 'scientific' everything that happens to agree with its particular prejudices, and to relegate to the limbo of human error all the evidence that appears from the other side. Another characteristic of this movement has been the flattery of authors who favour the views to be inculcated with such appellations as 'greatest living authority', 'foremost scientist', 'the wise physician of today, who is abreast of the modern investigations concerning the drug', 'author of great prominence', 'most skilled in his profession', 'eminent scholar' etc." (Billings 1903 p. 23).

Clearly, in the Committee of Fifty's view, the Hunt-WCTU depiction of the dangers of alcohol suffered from the not-inconsiderable disadvantage of being wrong. Today, reading the florid language used by Hunt et-al in pursuit of their ideological obsessions, it is difficult not to conclude that these were the rants of fundamentally unhappy people.

THE ANTI-SALOON LEAGUE AND THE AMERICAN ISSUE PUBLISHING COMPANY

Not content with attempts to proselytise the anti-alcohol cause amongst school children and college students, the temperance movement sought to influence adult American public opinion via pressure politics and the printing press. In 1893 the Anti-Saloon League was formed and in 1909 it established the American Issue Publishing Company.

THE ANTI-SALOON LEAGUE

The Anti-Saloon League was formed on May 24th 1893 by a small number of professors, preachers and small business owners. They met in the library of Oberlin College, Ohio, with the immediate purpose of discussing how to turn Ohio dry.

Their foremost founding member was the Reverend Howard Hyde Russell. Formerly a lawyer, Russell underwent religious conversion and had attended seminary at Oberlin College. By the time of this meeting he was an established Congregationalist pastor who had campaigned for 'local option' – the WCTU campaign for city and state-wide prohibition. He'd witnessed the split in the WCTU between those who wanted it to be a single-issue organisation and those who wanted to broaden out its campaigning appeal. He was also witness to the complete failure of the Prohibition Party to gain any electoral traction, and was certain they were never going to send a man to the White House. What remained of the pre-Civil War temperance organisations, such as the American Temperance Society, lacked political proficiency and Russle regarded them merely as pamphleteers.

By focussing on the saloon, rather than drinking *per se*, the Anti-Saloon League had hit on a popular cause of concern. By all accounts American saloons were often pretty grim places; and whilst the pseudo-science of Mary Hanchet-Hunt might frighten the children, highlighting the state of the saloon as a social institution spoke to the experience of ordinary, adult Americans and was a much more successful tactic in marshalling support. Those who enjoyed a drink at home, or who tippled at family or social events were persuaded that the League wasn't anti-alcohol, they were anti-saloon.

This was pure sophistry. The League's Charter explicitly set out its strategy:

"The object of the League is the extermination of the beverage liquor traffic, for the accomplishing of which the alliance of all who are in harmony with this object are invited. The League pledges itself to avoid affiliation with any political party as such and to maintain an attitude of strict neutrality on all questions of public policy not directly and immediately concerned with the traffic in strong drink."

Russell fashioned the Anti-Saloon League into a non-partisan, single-issue political lobbying group that developed branches across the United States, and it worked with churches to put pressure on the established political parties to promote the prohibition of alcohol. It drew its initial support from the Protestant churches in rural areas and in the South. And it was pragmatic in its approach. Unlike the Prohibition Party, it was non-partisan;

unlike the WCTU, it wasn't led by a controversial suffragette of eclectic political views and it did not discriminate against men; unlike democratic organisations, it operated from the top down and unlike the Ku Klux Klan it did not engage in the enforcement of prohibition laws.

THE AMERICAN ISSUE PUBLISHING COMPANY

The establishment of the American Issue Publishing Company on a site gifted by the citizens of Westerville, Ohio led to the construction of the printing plant which opened in June 1909. The output of anti-alcohol propaganda was prodigious. The presses operated 24 hours a day and employed around 200 people. Within three years of its establishment the publishing house was producing a quarter of a billion (250,000,000) book pages per month. The quantity increased annually. This level of publication dwarfed that of the National Temperance Society's publishing house, which took over 50 years to produce a mere one billion pages.

The American Issue Publishing Company published books on temperance as well as periodical magazines including the American Issue, the American Patriot, the New Republic, the Scientific Temperance Journal, the National Daily, the Worker, the Intercollegiate Statesman and the International Student. The titles and content of these journals give a clear indication of the symbolism and appeal of the temperance crusade for those involved in it: nativist, traditionalist, patriotic, Protestant, and totally paranoid.

The sheer volume of output from prohibitionist presses was bound to influence the culture, and public attitude to alcohol, and therefore the political attitudes of politicians who ride on public opinion. But if the printed word was not enough, the cause threw up leaders whose personal and political output was no less prodigious. Enter one Wayne Wheeler.

WAYNE WHEELER

Wayne Bidwell Wheeler was a prohibitionist and the de facto leader of the Anti-Saloon League. Like other temperance movement figures his attitude to alcohol became fixed early in his life by childhood experiences, which evidently left a big impression on him. Two incidents in particular are cited by historians of the time: while working as a boy on his family's farm his leg was injured by a drunken farm hand wielding a pitchfork, and he also witnessed another drunken person frighten his mother and sister.

Wayne Wheeler - De-Facto leader of the Anti-Saloon League

Like many American temperance leaders he was well-educated and articulate. After his high school graduation he taught for two years before seeking to further his education by entering Oberlin College, in Ohio. In 1894 he received his BA and immediately accepted employment as an organiser for the Anti-Saloon League. But he continued his studies at Western Reserve Law School, from which he received his LLB in 1898. He was then appointed attorney for the League to which he devoted the rest of his life.

Wheeler was a brilliant, if unscrupulous, leader. He is credited with inventing what today we would call pressure politics. At the time it became known as 'Wheelerism' and the term 'wheeling and dealing' is said to derive from the political tactics of Wayne Wheeler.

Under Wheeler's leadership the League focussed entirely on the achievement of alcohol prohibition. It supported or opposed candidates for public office on the basis of their position in relation to the prohibition of alcohol, regardless of their political views on anything else. Republican or Democrat: it didn't matter. What mattered is whether you were 'wet' or 'dry'.

The Anti-Saloon League worked with the mainstream political parties rather than backing the smaller Prohibition Party. The premise was simple: when people voted in congressional or presidential elections, they were participating in a process that led to the formation of a government. Electors made their choice on a range of issues. They were never going to vote-in a presidential candidate whose political platform had but one plank. So the Anti-Saloon League merely sought to ensure that as many politicians as possible, from across the political spectrum, included a prohibitionist plank in their electoral platform. To further the cause Wheeler organised the supporters of abstinence as a block vote.

According to his biographer:

"Wayne Wheeler controlled six congresses, dictated to two presidents of the United States, directed legislation in most States of the Union, picked the candidates for the more important elective state and federal offices, held the balance of power in both Republican and Democratic parties, distributed more patronage than any dozen other men, supervised a federal bureau from outside without federal authority, and was recognized by friend and foe alike as the most masterful and powerful single individual in the United States." *(Steuart, p. 11)*

Increasingly, the League's membership criticised Wheeler's alignment with religious bigots and groups. He also advocated illegal actions in enforcing prohibition, such as the addition of poisonous substances to industrial alcohol to prevent its consumption as beverage, arguing that "the government is under no obligation to furnish people with alcohol that is drinkable when the Constitution prohibits it. The person who drinks this industrial alcohol is committing a deliberate suicide."

Wayne Wheeler claimed to have written the National Prohibition Enforcement Act, known as the 'Volstead Act' after Congressman Andrew Volstead, who was the official author and who guided it through congress. Congressman Volstead repeatedly denied this claim, but there is little doubt that Wheeler was highly influential in its drafting.

Despite being a person with an abrasive personality who, by all accounts, could have written a book entitled "How to Lose Friends and Alienate People", Wheeler was a major player and made the Anti-Saloon League the foremost proponent of prohibition in the United States and a staunch defender of it once achieved. But Wheeler wasn't the only colourful agitator for prohibition. The WCTU had its own candidate for the accolade of Most Hateful Person – Carrie A. Moore née Carry A. Nation.

HATCHETATION!

Whilst Frances E. Willard may have been regarded by some as a Renaissance woman, not even her greatest admirers would have described Carrie Amelia Moore in such a way. However, Moore was undoubtedly the most colourful activist member of the WCTU. Born in Kentucky in 1846, the daughter of slave owners George and Mary Campbell Moore, she had an unsettled childhood and during her teenage years her family frequently moved about because of the Civil War.

In 1866 at the age of 20, having settled in Holden, Missouri, she entered into her first marriage to Dr Charles Gloyd. She separated from Gloyd shortly before she gave birth to their daughter, Charlien, on September 27th 1868. She was widowed less than a year later when her husband, a chronic alcoholic, died in 1869. Her husband's death made her passionate about fighting the liquor trade.

She had better luck in 1874 when she met and married a lawyer and Methodist preacher named David Nation, a man 20 years her senior, who had a daughter of his own, Lola, from a previous marriage. Although the official records show her given name as 'Carrie', the family Bible refers to her as 'Carry'. It wasn't lost on her that her married name 'Carry A. Nation' had a certain ring to it and she later had it registered as a trademark in Kansas. The family purchased a 1,700 acre cotton plantation on the San Bernard River in Brazoria County, Texas. Since neither of them knew much about farming this was a failure and they sold up and moved to Medicine Lodge, Kansas in 1879. David Nation preached at a local Christian church and Carry ran a successful hotel there.

She also started the Medicine Lodge chapter of the WCTU and began campaigning for the enforcement of Kansas' ban on sales of beverage alcohol. At first she followed the usual methods employed by WCTU activists – trying to shame saloon keepers with prayer vigils and hymn-singing. But she quickly became disillusioned with the outcomes of this form of activism. She began to pray to God for inspiration and on June the 5th 1899 she claims to have received a heavenly vision. She described her vision thus:

"The next morning I was awakened by a voice that seemed to me to be speaking in my heart, these words, 'go to Iowa' and my hands were lifted and thrown down and the words 'I'll stand by you'. The words 'go to Iowa' were spoken in a murmuring, musical tone low and soft, but 'I'll stand by you' was very clear, positive and emphatic. I was impressed with a great inspiration, the interpretation was very plain, it was this: 'take something in your hands, and throw at these places in Kiowa and smash them' ". (*Kansas Historical Society, Carry's Inspiration for Smashing*).

Carry went to Iowa where she used rocks to smash the stock of three local saloons. She continued her campaign of destruction and her fame grew along with her arrest record, and after she led a raid in Wichita her husband jokingly suggested that next time she should carry a hatchet for maximum damage. So she took him at his word.

Carry Nation has been described as a big woman, almost six feet in height and weighing around twelve and a half stone. However, photographs of her standing next to others suggests that she was quite a small lady. She described herself as "a bulldog running along at the feet of Jesus, barking at what he doesn't like." (*Kevan McQueen, 2001, Carrie Nation: Militant Prohibitionist*). Her party piece became entering saloons and bars with a hatchet and smashing them up. She referred to this form of agitation as "hatchetation".

Carry A. Nation

WCTU Activist

—

During her campaign of 'hatchetation' she didn't have it all her own way. She was arrested and jailed at least 30 times, received a black eye from a saloon keeper's wife, was attacked by prostitutes who pelted her with eggs, hit with a chair by a saloon-keeper who recognised her walking down the street, and knocked to the ground by a customer in one saloon when she slapped a cigarette out of his mouth. Reportedly she came close to being lynched in Wichita and was lucky to escape with her life on a number of other occasions.

In August 1901, after 27 years of marriage, her husband filed for divorce. One can only marvel at the man's stoical forbearance, but finally, he'd had enough and charged that his wife had neglected her family, abandoned the family home and held him up to public ridicule.

Over the following eight years Carry continued her exploits and rose to national fame. In 1903 she appeared in a vaudeville theatre production in which she played an obsessive saloon-smasher – a role which didn't exactly test her acting talent. She became something of a caricature of herself out of the necessity to pay an unending stream of fines and claims for damages; she sold souvenir hatchets and in 1904 published *The Use and Need of the Life of Carry A. Nation* – a book that sold over 60,000 copies.

Her one solid achievement appears to have been her role in getting prohibition written into the constitution of the newly inaugurated State of Oklahoma. This achievement in 1907 presaged the revival of statewide prohibition in America. Shortly after this she visited Britain where she made appearances in London's music halls, spoke to various packed meetings and, despite now being in her sixties, she found enough time and energy to smash up a pub in Newcastle-upon-Tyne. She proceeded north to Glasgow where she was greeted by a mob of some 3,000 no-nonsense Glaswegians from whom she was rescued by the police.

When she returned to America she sold her hatchets and bought a farm in Arkansas that she named Hatchet Hall. Two years later, in June 1911 whilst delivering a speech in a park in Eureka Springs, she suffered a heart attack and was taken to a hospital in Leavenworth where she died of heart failure. Carry Nation was buried in an unmarked grave in the Belton City Cemetary in Missouri, although the WCTU later erected a stone inscribed "Faithful to the Cause of Prohibition, She Hath Done What She Could." It is reported that "I have done what I could" were her last words. The stone carried her name: "Carry A. Nation." Her former home in Medicine Lodge was bought by the WCTU in the 1950s and was declared a US National Historic Landmark in 1976.

Perhaps the most humorous testament to her life's work appeared during her lifetime in the form of a notice that was displayed in thousands of saloons across America. It read: "All Nations Welcome – Except Carry!" No doubt she took it as a compliment.

THE RUN-UP TO PROHIBITION

Carry Nation never lived to see the enactment of national prohibition, but by the early 1900s the Anti-Saloon League's agitation was beginning to achieve critical mass. The relentless anti-alcohol propaganda of the American Issue Publishing Company, combined with the pressure politics of Wayne Wheeler, was finally bearing fruit. By 1906 over a third of the population of the United States lived in 'dry territory'. Regardless of whether the prohibition was enforced or not, this was a big platform from which to push for the constitutional amendment needed to enact prohibition nationwide.

Nevertheless, states, and towns and counties within them, continued to reject 'local option' prohibitions. Even where prohibition had been tried it was then sometimes repealed. An example of this was South Dakota, which repealed its dry laws in 1897 after eight years.

The progress made by the Anti-Saloon League was made easier by the supine inaction of the alcohol industry itself. The attitude seemed to be one of just 'take it on the chin'. But when, in 1907, the Anti-Saloon League made a concerted attempt to achieve prohibition in the states where it had strongest support – Alabama, Oklahoma, Tennessee, Georgia and North and South Carolina - the sheer scale of this push elicited a belated response from the alcohol industry. The distillers formed the National Model License League, which was an attempt to juxtapose the reform of the saloon as an alternative to its closure.

The National Model License League declared itself in favour of true temperance – moderate drinking – and agitated for tougher licensing and regulation. Meanwhile, the historical split between distillers and brewers continued to dog attempts to present a united front in the face of the temperance threat. The brewers, who owned most of the saloons, refused to join the National Model License League, and so the industry was ill-prepared for the decisive battle in the State of Ohio.

THE BATTLE FOR OHIO

Ohio had huge symbolic importance. It was the state that had hosted Dr Diocletian Lewis's sermon that gave rise to the original Ohio Women's Crusade and the formation of the WCTU. It was also the home of the brewers and the Baptists. Politically, it was widely regarded as a bellwether state in terms of public opinion.

The Anti-Saloon League was able to get state-wide prohibition on the ballot paper in Ohio no less than four times between 1914 and 1918. They lost three times – in 1914 and 1915 and then again in 1917 by the tightest of margins, just 1,137 out of a million votes cast. In 1918, when they finally won the ballot, the vote had shifted to just over 51% in favour. This tight result demonstrated just what a divisive issue alcohol was and how split the American people were on the issue.

But even before the Ohio ballots it was clear that growing distrust of the immigrant population caused opposition to alcohol to become more pronounced as the economic, political, and social power of the cities developed. And war was coming. This gave a strong impetus to the anti-German sentiment which shook the country in a mood of anticipation before WWI. Since most of the breweries were German-owned, they became the scapegoats.

The United States Brewers Association misread the prevailing public mood and associated itself with the German-American Alliance to oppose the temperance advocates and defend 'German kultur' in the United States.

The war gave the prohibition cause new ammunition. Literature depicted brewers and licensed retailers as treacherously stabbing American soldiers in the back. Raw materials and labour were being diverted from the war effort to an industry which debilitated the nation's capacity to defend itself. It was urged that wartime prohibition would stop the waste of grain and molasses and would remove a handicap on workers' efficiency.

"Liquor is a menace to patriotism because it puts beer before country," preached Wayne Wheeler. In this atmosphere the Wartime Prohibition Act was passed in 1918. It followed a series of federal laws such as the Wilson Original Packages Act and the Webb-Kenyon Act, attempts to protect dry states from their wet neighbours.

The Wilson Original Packages Act was passed on August 8, 1890, and provided that all intoxicating beverages shipped interstate would be subject to the laws of the destination state upon arrival. No mechanism for federal enforcement was provided.

The Webb-Kenyon Act, enacted March 1st, 1913, was intended to reinforce the 1890 Act by making it a violation of federal law to ship an intoxicating beverage interstate with the intent that it be used or sold in any manner in violation of the laws of the destination state. The lack of federal enforcement rendered the statute virtually meaningless.

The Reed Amendment, enacted four years later, provided a fine of $1,000 for transporting liquor into a dry state, again with no greater effect.

None of the earlier acts met with substantial success in curbing the flow of liquor into dry regions, but they did mark a change in federal policy. Formerly liquor laws were designed solely to produce federal revenue; Congress now began to understand the role it could play in the regulation of alcohol consumption.

This role was initially forced upon a reluctant Congress. Indeed, the government had passed-up numerous previous opportunities to involve itself in the temperance movement. The particular part it was to play was forecast by the Sons of Temperance who, as far back as 1856, declared themselves for national constitutional prohibition.

Twenty years later in 1876, Congressman Henry Blair of New Hampshire introduced a prohibition amendment to the Constitution for the first time in Congress. As a senator, he introduced another such resolution in 1885, along with Senator Preston Plum of Kansas. After consideration by the

Senate Committee on Education, the bill was reported-out favourably and placed on the Senate Calendar in 1886. Nevertheless, no action resulted.

In the meantime, states continued the struggle between the wets and the dries, with increasing success for the temperance advocates. By 1913, nine states were under state-wide prohibition. In 31 other states, local option laws were in effect; by means of these and other regulatory schemes, more than 50% of the United States population was then under prohibition.

The national constitutional campaign was resumed in earnest in 1913 when the Anti-Saloon League went on record at its 15th National Convention in favour of immediate prosecution of the objective of constitutional amendment.

The National Temperance Council, founded at the same time, co-ordinated the activities of numerous temperance organisations with the same objective. In 1913, the demands of the League were formally presented to Congress by the Committee of 1,000. The introduction of federal income tax in the same year freed the federal government of its reliance on alcohol and tobacco as its main source of tax revenue. The scene was set for constitutional change.

The measure was then introduced in the House by Congressman Thompson and in the Senate by Senator Sheppard. The following year, the first joint resolution failed to secure the necessary two thirds majority required for submission of a constitutional amendment to the states. A second resolution was submitted in 1915 and favourably considered by the Judiciary Committees of both houses, but neither ever came to a vote.

Ultimately, in 1917, the resolution to prohibit the manufacture, sale, transportation or importation of alcoholic beverages in the United States was approved by Congress and sent to the states for ratification.

It took only one year and eight days for the 18th Amendment to secure the necessary ratification. On January 8th, 1918, Mississippi proudly became the first state to ratify, and on January 16th, 1919, Nebraska completed the job as the 36th state. By the end of February 1919, there remained only three states still holding out: New Jersey, Connecticut, and Rhode Island.

October 28th, 1919, was the day that Congress enacted the National Prohibition Act, known as the 'Volstead Act' after the Congressman who drafted it and guided it through the legislative process, with the intent to give effect to the new constitutional amendment. Officially, prohibition was to begin on January 17th, 1920.

WAS PROHIBITION A SUCCESS?

It is beyond the scope of this book to give a detailed history of prohibition itself, but it lasted until repeal of the 18th Amendment in 1933. The 18th Amendment retains the distinction of being the only amendment to the American Constitution to have been repealed. As a postscript it is nevertheless worthwhile to consider why it was finally and decisively rejected by the American people.

The early experience of the Prohibition era gave the government a taste of what was to come. In the three months before the 18th Amendment took effect, liquor worth half a million dollars (at 1920 prices) was stolen from Government warehouses. By midsummer of 1920, federal courts in Chicago were overwhelmed with some 600 pending liquor violation trials. Within three years, 30 prohibition agents were killed whilst on active service.

Other statistics demonstrated the increasing volume of the bootleg trade. According to the US Internal Revenue Service in 1921 95,933 illicit distilleries, stills, still works and fermenters were seized. In 1925, the total jumped to 172,537 and up to 282,122 in 1930. In connection with these seizures, 34,175 persons were arrested in 1921; by 1925, the number had risen to 62,747 and to a high in 1928 of 75,307. Concurrently, convictions for liquor offences in federal courts rose from 35,000 in 1923 to 61,383 in 1932.

Prohibition Era Village Still

The law could not quell the continuing demand for beverage alcohol. Thus, where legal enterprises could no longer supply the demand, an illicit traffic developed, from the point of manufacture to consumption. The institution of the speakeasy replaced the institution of the saloon. Estimates of the number of speakeasies throughout the United States ranged from 200,000 to 500,000.

Writers of this period point out that the law was circumvented by various means. Although there may have been legitimate, medicinal purposes for whiskey, or at least it was believed this was so at the time, the practice of obtaining a medical prescription for the illegal substance was abused, just as medical prescriptions for marijuana are abused in California and other states today. It is estimated that doctors earned $40 million in 1928 alone by writing prescriptions for whiskey.

The legal system was equally evasive; the courts convicted about seven percent of those charged with liquor violations (*Sinclair, 1962: 193-195; Dobyns, 1940: 292*). The exception for sacramental wine, protected under the Volstead Act, also invited abuse. In 1925, the Department of Research and Education of the Federal Council of the Churches of Christ reported that:

"The withdrawal of wine on permit from bonded warehouses for sacramental purposes amounted in round figures to 2,139,000 gallons in the fiscal year 1922; 2,503,500 gallons in 1923; and 2,944,700 gallons in 1924. There is no way of knowing what the legitimate consumption of fermented sacramental wine is, but it is clear that the legitimate demand does not increase by 800,000 gallons in two years."

The smuggling trade was revived with new vigour and new incentives. Rum-runners, often under foreign flags, brought liquor into the country from Belgium and Holland. In 1923, there were 134 seizures of such vessels. The following year, 236 were apprehended. With fewer risks, liquor was readily smuggled across the Canadian border. One way or the other, the Department of Commerce estimated that, as of 1924, liquor valued at approximately $40 million was entering the United States annually.

The legal manufacture of 'near-beer' (beer up to 1.2% ABV), and industrial alcohol provided other opportunities for diversion from licit channels, while the salvage of the California grape industry under section 29 of the Volstead Act authorised the home production of fermented fruit juices. Although this section was allegedly inserted to save the vinegar industry and the hard cider of America's farmers, it was welcomed by home wine-makers as well. In the spirit of co-operation, the grape growers even produced a type of grape jelly suggestively called "Vine-go" which, with the addition of water, could make a strong wine within two months.

One of the great ironies of the Prohibition era was the fact, noted by the Wickersham Commission, that women happily took to drink during the experimental decade. As the counterpart of the WCTU, the Women's Organization for National Prohibition Reform was founded, stating in its declaration of principles that Prohibition was wrong in principle and "disastrous in consequences in the hypocrisy, the corruption, the tragic loss of life and the appalling increase of crime which has attended the abortive attempt to enforce it."

The lasting legacy of national prohibition is that the minimum age for purchasing alcohol is 21 years, but the voting age is 18. Thus we still have partial prohibition in that, outside of the Islamic world, the United States is the only country to ban a category of adults (18 to 20 year-olds) from buying alcohol.

Did prohibition succeed? Well, firstly, if the point of banning something is to stop it happening – it didn't. Millions of Americans continued to buy and drink alcohol. The attempt to legally suppress the mass market failed completely. However, for such large-scale flouting of the law to happen required the corruption of public officials on a massive scale. Police officers, court officials, judges and congressmen all had to be bribed to turn a 'blind eye'. Organised crime and the rise of mafia in the United States was therefore a product of National Prohibition.

The murder rate increased fivefold as rival gangsters battled it out in turf wars – the St Valentine's Day Massacre is just one of the more infamous examples. The Klu Klux Klan was a supporter of Prohibition and many a gun battle took place between them and the mob over the delivery of alcohol!

Al Capone- organised bootlegging

Frank Nitti- battled the KKK

Less well known is that prohibition led to a huge increase in the trafficking of women for prostitution. Prohibition separated men from women. Women drinkers preferred to get together in one another's homes. Men preferred to visit illegal bars - 'Speakeasies' - where they met women trafficked for prostitution by organised crime. This in turn led to an increased incidence of sexually transmitted diseases – a very serious matter in a society that had yet to discover penicillin.

When you look at the attempts by the alcophobes and water drinkers of our latter-day neo-prohibitionist movement to restrict alcohol sales you have to wonder what the end-game is. If in their secret hearts they really hanker after the good-old-days of prohibition, they, and we, would be well advised to look at what really happened the last time government attempted to socially engineer the sober society. The lasting lesson of America's 'noble experiment' is that you can't suppress a mass market in an open society.

Celebrating the end of Prohibition

Chapter 2:

UK Temperance and Licensing

In this chapter I trace the history of the Temperance movement in the UK that culminated in a failed attempt by the Liberal Government of Henry Campbell-Bannerman and his Chancellor Herbert Asquith to nationalise the pub industry in 1908, and at the partial nationalisation that took place at the outset of WWI.

I trace the early regulation of alcohol in the UK and the legislative attempts, mostly characterised by benign paternalism, to socially engineer the sober society. The comparison with US and UK responses on the 'alcohol issue' is made, and the religious and social symbolism examined.

HISTORICAL AND CULTURAL PERSPECTIVES

The British love of drink is one of the great historical truisms. As early as the 8th century, the missionary Saint Boniface was writing to Cuthbert, Archbishop of Canterbury, to complain: "In your dioceses the vice of drunkenness is too frequent. This is an evil peculiar to pagans and to our race. Neither the Franks nor the Gauls nor the Lombards nor the Romans nor the Greeks commit it." *(Tristram Hunt, Building Jerusalem: The Rise and Fall of the Victorian City).*

EARLY LEGAL REGULATION OF ALCOHOL

It only took around 700 years for this concern to be recognised by legal regulation. In 1495 Henry VII, then leading England out of medieval confusion, enacted the first statute governing the conduct of alehouses. This statute empowered local justices to take financial sureties from the keepers of alehouses as a guarantee of their good conduct. Judges of Assize were given the power to suppress alehouses that were, in their view, unnecessary. Just over half a century later, in 1552, a proper system was created for licensing alehouses for the first time. Licensees were required to recognise their responsibility for running an orderly house, unlawful games were prohibited, and drunkenness was outlawed.

Similarly, fear over the effects of excessive drinking is woven into our cultural fabric. In the 18th century the great moral panic was gin. In 1742 a population barely a tenth the size of todays' consumed 19 million gallons of gin - ten times as much as is drunk today. William Hogarth graphically depicted these concerns in his 1751 engraving 'Gin Lane', with its allegorical litany of drunken rioting, collapsing family bonds and endemic poverty. Gin Lane was of course located in London, and the dangers of heavy drinking have traditionally been linked in the public consciousness with urban culture.

THE GIN CRAZE

Public and political concern over the consequences of excessive alcohol use preceded the formal creation of the various temperance groups that sprang up in the 1830s. The most vivid example of this came to be known as the 'Gin Craze'. Gin became popular in England following the accession of William of Orange in 1688. It was regarded as patriotic to drink gin rather than French brandy because, notwithstanding the fact that a Dutch physician Franciscus Sylvius is popularly credited with its invention in the mid-17th century, it was distilled in London, whereas brandy was imported from France. The popularity of gin grew at a time when there was growing political and religious conflict between Britain and France.

Over a decade, starting in 1689, the government passed numerous laws restricting imports of brandy and encouraging English gin production. The monopoly of the London Guild of Distillers was broken in 1690 and this freed-up the market in gin distillation. London as the locus of gin distillation is still reflected in gin products available today, where references are made on gin bottle labels to 'London Dry Gin'. Anti-French economic protectionism was thus a major factor in starting the 'Gin Craze' of the first half of the 18th century. Disposable income grew as a result of food prices falling and cheap gin became available for discretionary spend by the masses. Magistrates began vociferously to complain that gin consumption by the lower classes was the cause of much of the crime, vice and debauchery that they had to deal with at that time.

Parliament's response was to pass five major Acts in 1729, 1736, 1743, 1747 and 1751 – all designed to control the consumption of gin. The 1736 Act added a tax of 20 shillings a gallon on all retail spirits and the licensees of alehouses were required to take out an annually renewable licence at a cost of £50 a year - a princely sum in 1736 - in order legally to sell gin. This was an early attempt to use taxation to raise price and thereby reduce consumption, but the English drinking classes were not to be so easily deterred! The legislation failed miserably – only two licences were ever taken out and the gin trade therefore became effectively illegal; to such an extent that informers were offered £5 rewards to reveal the location of illegal gin shops. But the 1736 Act was repealed in 1743 following mass riots and violence directed towards informants.

By 1743 the people of England were drinking an average of over three gallons of gin per head of population annually. Demands grew for more effective controls but the gin craze began to subside after the Gin Act 1751 which lowered the annual licence fee, thereby encouraging a legal trade that could more effectively be controlled (and taxed). Gin retailing was encouraged to go up-market, and it became more 'respectable' as a consequence of the 1751 Act requirement that gin retailers operate from premises which were rented for at least £10 a year. But, beyond the ineffectual meddling of legislators, wider changes to the economic landscape began to be felt. Rises in the price of grain, poor harvests, falling wages and increased food prices lowered discretionary spend and the gin craze was pretty much over by 1757.

THE GIN PALACE

There was a resurgence of gin drinking just before and during the Victorian era that arose with changes to legislation and the requirement that gin shops had to be licensed to sell ale and wine. The gin shops gradually became larger and plusher. Far from trying to achieve a 'home-away-from-home' feel, the object was to create an escape from the poverty of Victorian home life for the mass of the poor, industrial proletariat. The 'gin palace' first appeared in the late 1820s. The first two that were built in London were Thompson and Fearon's in Holborn and Weller's in Old Street. Gin palaces were lit by gas lamps, and characterised by etched glass, panelled walls and were expensively fitted out. The upper classes regarded them as vulgar, but the working class poor of 19th century London flocked to them.

Very few of the original gin palaces survive, although later Victorian pubs are clearly modelled on them. Examples include the Café Royal in Edinburgh, the Horseshoe Bar in Glasgow, The Red Lion in Duke of York Street and the Salisbury in St Martin's Lane, both in London. Another magnificent example of this gin-palace style of pub is the Philharmonic Dining Rooms in Liverpool.

Philharmonic Dining Rooms, Liverpool

EARLY EXAMPLES OF MORAL PANIC

The government's response to the Gin Craze, and later to the rise of the gin palaces, provides us with early examples of moral panic. What government was responding to was a series of issues constructed by the media of the day that drew their power not simply from the inherent features of what they described, but from their capacity to mediate a package of wider social anxieties; these anxieties included concerns about the impact of rapid urbanisation on law and order; the growth of disposable income amongst the working class, and how their patterns of alcohol consumption would impact on the work ethic and the responsibilities of hearth and home; a widespread anxiety about family breakdown and maternal neglect of children; xenophobia – particularly in relation to the French; and a general anxiety about the failure of government to grasp the seriousness of the problems facing society, or to fashion remedies.

The campaign to reduce the consumption of gin was led by middle-class Londoners whose social concerns were exemplified by artist and engraver William Hogarth. These people were deeply concerned about the moral health of society, critical of the debauched lifestyle of the landed aristocracy and their lack of interest in solving the problems that beset the society around them. Hogarth's prints, and later those of teetotaller George Cruikshank, provided the social commentaries of their day.

There can't be a moral panic without a media that provides the oxygen of publicity needed to spread it. There had been a surge of printing and publishing when the Licensing Act lapsed in 1695. This particular Licensing Act had nothing to do with licensing alcohol, but was the Act that required the licensing of books and publications and its lapse created the basis of the free press. The emergence of a permanent newspaper press quickly followed.

Hogarth's 'Gin Lane' and 'Beer Street' were a part of this print revolution and were produced and sold at low prices to make them affordable to the middle and lower middle-class. The publication of these two prints in 1751 raised the perennial cry of the middle-class moral reformer 'something must be done!' And so the government felt compelled to take legislative action. The Gin Craze can therefore be characterised as an early example of a media-driven moral panic.

Hogarth's Beer Street   *Hogarth's Gin Lane*

TEMPERANCE AND THE RISE OF VICTORIAN MORALISM

The industrialisation of early 19th century Britain created rapid urbanisation, and caused an influx of thousands of country people into London and the growing cities of northern England. Instant escape from the misery of grinding poverty and exploitation was to be found in the bottle! The gin palaces of 19th century Britain sold alcohol on an industrial scale. These establishments are easily recognisable as the forerunners of today's super-pubs, geared up for mass-volume drinking.

The government's response was to champion the virtue of beer as more wholesome refreshment. Hogarth's engraving 'Beer Street', published much earlier, had celebrated its healthy effects. In 1830, nearly 80 years later, the government passed the Beer Act that allowed any householder with a two-guinea licence to sell ale and porter - but not wine or spirits. The number of beer shops exploded and the pub began to take its place as a central part of working class culture.

The impact of legislation on excessive consumption merely changed what was drunk – from gin to beer; and where it was drunk – from city-centre gin palaces to suburban beer shops. But it didn't significantly impact on excessive consumption itself. By the mid-1870s alcohol consumption reached a peak with 344 gallons of beer consumed per individual, per year *(Salvation Army pamphlet Darkest England and the Way Out, 1875)*. After the mid-1870s beer consumption began to decline. This decline happened not because of moral suasion or coercive legislative action, but because Victorian engineers were able to pipe clean, wholesome drinking water to the street hand-pump and then later into the home. So the drinking of 'small beer' – weak beer bought from street corner beer shops – subsided. An improvement to the material conditions of the working-class poor had a far greater impact than the hand-wringing concerns of middle-class moral reformers.

HUMANITARIANISM

The 19th century saw the first political expressions of middle-class conscience. Humanitarianism was the 'big idea' of the 19th century - the abolition of the slave trade in 1807, which was followed by its abolition throughout the Empire in 1833, happened before Victoria acceded to the throne in 1837. But later developments, such as the suffragettes and new laws governing child labour, exemplified how the Victorian merchant class sought to build the civic framework of the New Jerusalem. The Temperance Movement was also a product of this era. Imported from America at first to Ireland and then to Scotland, the Temperance Movement, with its evangelical denunciations of the evils of the 'demon drink', began to make its presence felt in Lancashire and Yorkshire during the 1840s.

Luminaries of the Temperance Society, such as Scottish artist George Cruikshank, whose older brother Isaac died from alcoholism, graphically illustrated the Victorian disapproval of alcohol. His masterpiece was a painting entitled "The Worship of Bacchus" depicting "The Drinking Customs of Society - showing how universally the intoxicating liquors are used on every social occasion from the cradle to the grave." This was later reproduced by him as an engraving. The original painting is still in the possession of the Whitbread brewing family and is a masterpiece of protest against the perceived evils of drink.

The Worship of Bacchus

Victorian capitalism needed its workers sober. Social alternatives to drinking, from tea parties to snooker clubs, were enthusiastically proffered while public pressure on brewers started to edge pubs out of city centres and into working class suburbs. Thomas Cook, the temperance campaigner and former Baptist preacher, went one stage further by taking the Victorian city's wayward classes on uplifting rural excursions. This tradition of restraint was not altogether upheld by his Club 18-30 package holiday descendants.

SCOTLAND: THE BIRTH OF THE UK TEMPERANCE MOVEMENT

I am grateful to Stephen McGowan, solicitor and Scottish temperance historian, for the account below of the early history of the temperance movement in Scotland:

"Scotland was, for many, the birth place of the temperance movement, with a number of local organisations being established in the late 18th and early 19th centuries, and for a long time remained in a state of diaspora until the formation of the Scottish Temperance League around 1844 in Glasgow. A separate organisation called the Scottish Permissive Bill Association was founded in 1858 and was heavily influenced by the prohibitionist state of Maine which had banned drink as early as 1852, the same year that the STL coined the word 'alcoholic' in their pamphlets and literature. The STL and the SPBA later became affiliated to the National Temperance Federation based in London, but as a result of success in lobbying for legislation, ultimately the Scottish groups amalgamated to become the Scottish Temperance Alliance.

The height of their success is arguably the passing of the Temperance (Scotland) Act 1913 which created local 'veto' powers to prevent and even close licensed premises. In the years following, when the temperance polls began after the Great War, the movement had several notable successes: most famously in the form of one Edwyn Scrymgeour.

Edwyn Scrymgeour is the only politician ever to be elected to Westminster as a temperance advocate and he was leader of the Scottish Prohibition Party. Mr Scrymgeour, a Dundonian, was a key figure in the Scottish temperance movement, establishing his party in 1901. He is perhaps most famous for defeating Winston Churchill, who was incumbent MP for Dundee in the general election of 1922. Churchill had been MP since 1908 and could not have been pleased that he was unseated by a prohibitionist.

The conflation of the temperance legislation and other historical events is perhaps not to be underestimated in assessing the vigour of the movement. With the onset of the Great War, the Liquor Control Board (established by the Defence of the Realm (Liquor Control) Regulations 1915) had in fact banned the sale of spirits in parts of Scotland from June 1916, primarily to curb drunkenness amongst the huge number of sailors in areas such as the northern naval bases at Scapa Flow and Invergordon. Although beer and wine were available, they were in short supply due to the war and so the people of Scotland experienced some years of temperance, of a sort, and with the vast majority of men of drinking age overseas at war, this 'period of calm' would have influenced the zeitgeist for those who would later support the temperance Acts and local veto system.

The Liquor Control Board also banned the practice known as 'treating' which might be more familiar to some readers if described as 'getting a round in'. The Liquor Control Board remained the 'licensing authority' in Gretna and Cromarty Firth areas until the Licensing (Abolition of State Management) Act 1971 came into force, which surprises many.

The local veto, under the Temperance (Scotland) Act 1913, which allowed local people to vote for 'No Change' (same number of licences), 'Limiting Resolution' (licences reduced by 25%) or 'No Licence' (no licences except for hotels and restaurants) was first attempted after the Great War and resulted in varying outcomes across Scotland and even legal action. The Clayson Committee, whose report of 1973 led to the Licensing (Scotland) Act 1976, found that there were 14 burghs, 10 wards and 36 temperance poll areas in the early 1920s after the first veto polls had occurred. Following a 'no licence' vote in Kirkintilloch in 1921, then part of the greater Glasgow and as such regulated by the then Glasgow licensing court (but now under the auspices of East Dunbartonshire Licensing Board), a group of licence holders launched a joint appeal which was heard in the Court of Session, and interdict granted, based on the efficacy and validity of the poll and using a variety of explanations that it had been unfair from everything to bad lighting to undue influence at the polling booths. A similar appeal in Wick was overturned in 1922 and ultimately a number of operators were forced to close having had their licence renewals refused because of the 'no licence' vote.

Perhaps unsurprisingly, the result of this was not that demand fizzled out, but that it was met in other ways, and to an extent some parts of Scotland started down the same road as the great American Prohibition endeavour: illegality. Ways were found to procure alcohol in those areas which had been euthanised of licences, and Scotland saw a rise in illicit stills and that great unlicensed venue, now of almost mythical proportions: the shebeen. Shebeens, perhaps best described as 'drinking dens', sprang up in various places in Scotland throughout the 1920s and 30s, and so great was their cultural impact that the word was still used in legislation until the 1970s.

Polls continued in Scotland after the Second World War but the movement was undermined, it is often suggested, by a sea-change in the outlook of a war-weary populace ready to enjoy pleasure and leisure pursuits instead. The polls survived longer than one might expect in Scotland - they remained a feature of the Licensing (Scotland) Act 1959 which was eventually repealed in 1977, although the reality was that the majority of this now diminishing number were all in the Greater Glasgow area and pertained to a large increase of new housing areas built after the Second World War to relieve the incredible congestion in the city centre. The polls then became not really about absolute prohibition but more to do with specific locality, and Clayson suggests they began to be used for purposes beyond that originally intended.

In addition to this, the commercial uncertainty that the polls created meant that brewers and publicans become leery of investing in their own premises, far less expanding and building new premises, for fear that a poll could result in refusal of their licence renewal. This Damocles sword created a situation of crumbling buildings, apathy and a workforce with lessening long-term views and curtailed pride and professionalism. With no compensation for the trader whose licence would be annulled, this also led to uninsurable businesses and a nation with a significant bar to capital investment, employment and growth in what we now call the hospitality sector.

The idea that the poll should be retained as an ultimate threat was described by the Clayson Committee as a "crude and unjust weapon." Clayson argued that a better approach was to foster best practice, encourage responsible businesses and sustainable growth. Commentators and policy makers in 2014 would do well to remember these lessons." *(Stephen McGowan, 'A short history of the temperance movement in Scotland and how this influenced alcohol policy').*

THE DEVELOPMENT OF THE TEMPERANCE MOVEMENT

The history of the temperance movement in the UK as a whole can be divided into three distinct phases. All three of these greatly affected the British working class. The first of these phases began in the 1830s when intemperance was beginning to be seen as a widespread problem. With the rise of industrialism, working hours became much more regulated than in the agricultural society and factory owners demanded punctual, alert and efficient factory workers. Previously, many working-class men had missed days off work due to their intoxication. However, as a result of industrialisation, this sort of behaviour was no longer acceptable because it hindered the work regimen of the factory. Soon, 'Saint Monday', an accepted day in agricultural society for men to recover from their 'hangovers', became an impediment to the efficiency of the new industrial factories and was no longer tolerated.

The earliest temperance societies in the UK were inspired by a Belfast professor of theology, and Presbyterian Church of Ireland Minister, the Reverend John Edgar. He famously poured his stock of whiskey out of his window in 1829. These early societies concentrated on campaigning against the drinking of spirits rather than beer or wine.

During the 1830s, at the beginning of the temperance reformation, twenty temperance societies were founded, totalling between two and three thousand members.

TEMPERANCE IN ENGLAND

In England the organised temperance movement was brought first to the northern industrial towns of Lancashire and Yorkshire in the 1830s by the middle class, who felt that they were fighting drunkenness out of Christian charity. The middle class, who saw intemperance as a problem solely in the working class, focused their efforts on eliminating hard liquor and sought to dramatically curb the widespread drunkenness which plagued Victorian society. They worked with clergymen and a few upper-class reformers to help working-class men control their drinking. Their goal was to enlist the help of those who drank only in moderation to fight against drunkenness, rather than to cure drunkards or prohibit all alcoholic beverages.

It was thought that the promotion of beer, which was believed to be less intoxicating than the hard liquor of the working class, would provide for social drinking rather than public intoxication. The Beer Act of 1830 began forty years of the free trade of beer and enabled any householder who paid two guineas to receive a licence to sell beer, cider or porter, but not wine or spirits.

It was believed that if beer was easily obtainable at an unlimited number of beer shops, people would choose to drink beer rather than gin, which was seen as more destructive and which was harder to obtain. In order to further encourage the sale of beer, in late 1830, the two guinea duty for the beer licence was eliminated, rendering beer even more accessible. Many working class men procured the licences so that they could profit from the sale of beer, and the street-corner beer shop, easily recognisable as the forerunner of the street-corner pub, proliferated.

When it became clear, however, that beer could be equally as intoxicating as the scorned drink, gin, temperance reformers realised that the Beer Act was a failure in controlling drunkenness and the second phase of the temperance movement began.

In 1832, those who fervently believed in the evil of alcohol called for an alcohol-free society and formed a group referring to themselves as 'teetotallers.' This group sought to convince the populace of Britain, and particularly England, that any consumption of alcoholic liquor was morally wrong. This alienated the middle class who had dominated the temperance movement during its first phase and who believed in controlling drunkenness rather than abolishing liquor. Whereas the temperance movement was founded by middle-class men seeking to improve the working class, the teetotal group was founded by seven working-class men under the leadership of Joseph Livesey.

JOSEPH LIVESEY AND 'TEETOTALISM'

Joseph Livesey was a temperance advocate who financed his campaigning from the profits he made from his cheese production business. He was first introduced to cheese as a food by a doctor whom he consulted over an ailment. It appears that this is what first alerted him to the idea that what we consumed had health impacts.

Joseph Livesey

The term 'teetotaller' is said to derive from a speech made in Preston by one of Livesey's followers, a plasterer named Richard 'Dickie' Turner. Dickie Turner suffered from a stammer and during this speech to the Preston Temperance Society in 1833 he asserted that his abstinence would be "reet down out-and-out t-t-total for ever and ever."

Livesey and his teetotal group took a pledge, promising never to consume any alcoholic beverages. This pledge was considered the cornerstone of the teetotal movement. Labelled the 'short pledge', it only required people to refrain from personal consumption. Later, the 'long pledge' was introduced; this forbade anyone under the pledge oath from serving alcohol in his or her home. For the middle class, this provided serious social problems because few socialites cared to dine in someone's home and not drink wine. Also, the 'long pledge' disallowed the giving or taking of sacramental wine.

In lieu of these strict rules, many middle-class people who supported temperance, but still wished to drink wine with their dinners, were not supportive of the teetotal movement. However, women at marrying age during this period were encouraged by teetotallers and non-teetotallers alike to only marry men who were teetotal.

Livesey opened the first temperance hotel in 1833 and in 1834 founded the first temperance publication, The Preston Temperance Advocate. This publication lasted only three years until its closure in 1837. In 1835 the British Association for the Promotion of Temperance was established.

UK TEMPERANCE AND THE CLASS STRUGGLE
Whereas 19th century temperance in America was driven by the Protestant middle class, and embraced a number of other issues, notably, women's suffrage, teetotalism in the UK gained traction amongst the industrial working class. From 1838 a mass working-class movement 'Chartism' that fought, amongst other things, for universal male suffrage, began to develop. 'Temperance Chartism' became an element of the broader temperance movement. Parliament refused to countenance votes for people who didn't own property, or for women. Working-class Temperance Chartists saw abstention from alcohol as a way of proving to the propertied classes that they were responsible enough, and had developed sufficient capacity for self-regulation, to be trusted with the vote.

Thus it is clear that whilst working-class temperance in the UK was a genuine attempt at self-improvement, the moral norms they aspired to were culturally owned by the Protestant middle class.

THE MOVEMENT BEGINS TO SPREAD
Meanwhile, temperance groups began to proliferate. In 1847 the Band of Hope was founded in Leeds. A constant theme of anti-alcohol campaigners,

right up to the present day, is the protection of children. The stated aim of the Band of Hope was to save working class children from the evils of alcohol. Members pledged to abstain "from all liquors of an intoxicating quality, whether ale, porter, wine or ardent spirits, except as medicine."

The American temperance movement didn't just influence Scotland, but also the UK movement as a whole. In 1851 the American state of Maine passed a law prohibiting the sale of alcohol except for "medicinal, mechanical or manufacturing purposes." Maine was the first 'dry state' and 12 other states then joined them. This inspired the formation of the United Kingdom Alliance, led by John Bartholomew Gough, to promote a similar law banning the sale of alcohol in the UK. Other temperance groups at this time still favoured moral suasion and viewed the United Kingdom Alliance's push for legal prohibition as hard-line and likely to create a backlash. This division limited the effectiveness of the UK temperance movement as a whole.

But, just as had happened in America, the view that it would not be possible to limit the use of alcohol by making an 'assimilative moral invitation' to the drinker alone began to gain support (Joseph Gusfield, Contested Meanings). Non-conformist groups, such as the Methodists, Quakers and the Salvation Army, which had been founded in 1864, continued to lobby parliament to restrict alcohol sales. In Wales Lady Llanover, whose religiosity embraced Methodist teaching, closed all public houses on her estate and became a passionate critic of alcoholic drinks.

'Good Templars' Wales

RESISTANCE BEGINS TO GROW

Meanwhile the temperance and abstinence campaigners didn't have it all their own way. The resistance of the populace to legislative attempts to restrict alcohol use was illustrated when the Sale of Beer Act 1854, which restricted Sunday opening hours, had to be repealed and a Sunday Trading Bill withdrawn, following widespread rioting that followed demonstrations in Hyde Park. Similarly, in 1859 a Prohibition Bill was overwhelmingly defeated in the House of Commons.

A closer examination of these events provides further evidence that concern about alcohol mediates wider social anxieties. The 'Wilson-Patten' or Sale of Beer Act 1854 was the outcome of pressure from supporters of the Lord's Day Observance Society (founded in 1831) which wanted strict observance of the Sabbath. It was presented to Parliament on the 13th July 1854 and received Royal Assent just over three weeks later on the 7th August.

The Act prohibited all drinking establishments from opening on Sunday's between 2.30 p.m. and 6.00 p.m. or after 10.00 p.m. The first the drinking public knew about this was when they turned up at their local and found it shut. Such was the level of grassroots discontent with this measure that over the following months petitions containing over half a million signatures were collected. However, this measure in itself did not provoke the famous mass protests that occurred in Hyde Park. The straw that broke the proverbial camel's back was the proposed Sunday Trading Bill.

Lord Robert Grosvenor MP (Middlesex) proposed a Bill that would have prevented Sunday trading in London. The proposal allowed for the continued trading of small shops and actually had the support of larger retailers, their employees and, of course, Evangelicals and Lord's Day observance supporters. Ranged against the measure were free-traders, free-thinkers and radicals and, most important and most numerical of all, shoppers.

In Victorian England the working week included Saturday, and Saturday evening was when most people got paid. Sunday was a day of rest and shopping; or, a day of rest and worshipping, depending on your predilection. Which of those you did tended to be a matter of social class. Although the Sunday Trading Bill would have placed no greater restriction on Sunday drinking than already imposed by the Sale of Beer Act, the two measures were seen by many Londoners as stemming from the same sentiment, and as representing an attack on the working class. In a society which had no refrigeration, how were working class people meant to manage if they couldn't buy food on a daily basis, particularly on the one day of rest allotted to them under the factory system?

The Times editorial of the 15th June 1855 read: "The rich, whose larders and whose cellars are well filled, can, of course, afford to turn up their eyes in pious horror at the enormities of the poor man's baked shoulder of mutton, and his pint of beer…" and concluded by saying "we have already cut down the poor man's Sunday at one end by our Public House Bill, and now we are attacking it from the other quarter. There will surely be a revulsion of feeling against all this."

THE HYDE PARK DEMONSTRATIONS OF 1855

The Thunderer had spoken! Supposedly the newspaper of the Establishment, when The Times pronounced on an issue it carried enormous influence in a society where the printed word was the sole means of mass communication. Within days posters began to appear in the capital calling for a mass demonstration to take place in Hyde Park on the 24th June. According to the Brewery History Journal's archives, it read:

"New Sunday Bill prohibiting newspapers, shaving, smoking, eating and drinking and all other kinds of recreation and nourishment both corporal and spiritual, which the poor people still enjoy at the present time. An open-air meeting of artisans, workers and 'the lower orders' generally of the capital will take place in Hyde Park on Sunday afternoon to see how religiously the aristocracy is observing the Sabbath and how anxious it is not to employ its servants and horses on that day, as Lord Robert Grosvenor said in his speech. The meeting is called for three o'clock on the right bank of the Serpentine, on the side towards Kensington Gardens. Come and bring your wives and children in order that they may profit by the example their 'betters' set them."

On the day of the demonstration some 200,000 people had gathered, chiefly members of the "lower classes" as The Times described them. James Bligh, a Chartist, presided over the meeting and began by expressing the hope that this would be a peaceful meeting at which people would express their opposition to the Bill in a lawful manner. At this point he was interrupted by one Inspector Banks, who was accompanied by "40 truncheon wielding constables." Bligh was politely told that because Hyde Park was not public property he couldn't hold a demonstration there and that he should move on. Quite how 40 constables were supposed to move 200,000 people if they didn't want to move is unclear, but Bligh, keen to keep the protest respectable, agreed to move the crowd to Oxford Market, where no such restrictions applied.

At this point a number of members of London's gentry entered the park for their Sunday promenade along the banks of the Serpentine. The Brewery History Journal quotes no less a figure than Karl Marx, who was an eye witness to the events, and who described them as:

"A procession of elegant ladies and gentlemen; 'commoners and Lords', in their high coaches-and-four with liveried lackeys in front and behind, joined, to be sure, by a few mounted venerables slightly under the weather from the effects of wine .... a babel of jeering, taunting, discordant ejaculations, in which no language is as rich as English, soon bore down on them from both sides."

Amid cries of "go to church!" and "walk, walk and let your horse rest, and your coachman go to church" the nobility was forced to alight and beat a hasty retreat. The police prevented any further speakers and despite the boisterous and irreverent attitude of the crowd it remained well behaved and no serious violence occurred. By 6.00 p.m. the crowd began to disperse.

Hyde Park Demo 1855

Within days a new notice appeared publicising a further meeting for the following Sunday, July 1st. This meeting was promptly banned by the Commissioner of the Metropolitan Police, but 150,000 people turned up in Hyde Park in defiance of the ban. The Times described them, the following day, as members of the "respectable class."

The police initially took a 'hands-off' approach and the meeting began with a number of speeches, one of which alleged that Lord Grosvenor had quit the capital the previous day, leaving 200 police officers to guard his house. However, during the speech some 40 police officers tried to arrest this speaker who nevertheless made good his escape. The police intervention upset the crowd, a number of whom began to shout "Down with the crushers!"

In a further provocation someone managed to get what the Daily Telegraph and Courier later described as "an enormous eel" out of the Serpentine and threw it at the police. Not only did the police arrest the eel, they also retaliated by wading into the crowd using their truncheons and a number of demonstrators were then arrested.

Whether the eel ended up getting jellied and fed to hungry police officers is not known, but with more cries of "go to church" being hurled at arriving gentlefolk, the police managed to fill seven cabriolets with arrested demonstrators who were taken to Vine Street police station. By 5:00 p.m. the mood became uglier and police reinforcements were sent for. About eight people were reported seriously injured and 104 arrested before the crowd eventually dispersed. The following day, 72 of those arrested appeared at Marlborough Street Court where a large crowd gathered, threw stones, and had to be dispersed with a police truncheon charge.

Reading the history of this today it is hard not to view it as a scene straight out of 'Carry on Constable', but the politicians of the day were profoundly shocked and Lord Grosvenor promptly stopped the passage of the Sunday Trading Bill through Parliament and shortly thereafter retired from public life.

Even this did not entirely quell public anger. The following Sunday, the 8th July, there was a third demonstration, albeit involving only around 4,000 people. 800 police officers were on duty and the military were on standby. There were cries of "Hyde Park butchers" from the crowd and a number of youths split off from the crowd and smashed windows in Belgrave Square, Upper Belgrave Street and Haton Street, Lord Grosvenor's house among them. Cries of "No Beer Bill", "No Bishops" and "Down with the Sabbatarians" were heard and in a 15 minute spree 749 panes of glass were broken to a value of some £400. A final gathering took place the following Sunday, but this was easily contained by the police.

The final legislative consequence of these demonstrations involved the government rowing back from the restrictions of the Sale of Beer Act 1854, and a further two and a half hours were added to drinking hours by legislative change that attracted little debate and no opposition.

Why was the government of the day so sensitive to these expressions of public anger? The series of European revolutions in 1848 would have been fresh in the memory of the British ruling class, and this encouraged government repression of popular demonstrations. It should also be remembered that the 19th century was a time of huge social and economic change. One aspect of this was population growth. Between 1801 and 1851 the population of England and Wales doubled - from 8.8 million to 17.9 million, and over 2 million people lived in London alone. Most of those attending the Hyde Park demonstrations were Londoners. To put 200,000 people on the streets, almost one in ten of the entire population of London, was therefore an impressive feat.

Karl Marx, whose publication of The Communist Manifesto in 1848 had caused a sensation, proclaimed that "the English revolution began yesterday in Hyde Park." *(Brewery History archive p. 118)*. Whilst Marx's prediction turned out to be somewhat premature, the fact remains that any large-scale eruption of working class discontent was something that the ruling class in and out of Parliament took very seriously, particularly if such outbreaks occurred in the capital. In an era in which capitalism was still nation-state based, and in which only the upper and middle classes were represented in Parliament, if the price of retaining private property was giving the working class a few more hours drinking time, it was clearly seen as one well worth paying.

THE LICENSING BILL AND THE 'PEOPLE'S PROTEST' OF 1908

Sunday trading and Sunday drinking restrictions were separate issues, but what they symbolised caused them to become conflated in the view of the public. Both were denounced in the 1855 protests. Subsequent to the Hyde Park demonstrations of 1855 questions were asked about who financed and organised them. It was never proven that the alcohol industry or alcoholic-drinks retailers were behind them, although undoubtedly they were the main beneficiaries of the legislative repeal that followed.

However, the drinks industry was very much to the fore in respect of the demonstration that took place on the 27th September 1908. The political background to this is complex and involved conflict between temperance campaigners and the brewers that had gone on for nearly a decade prior to 1908.

In 1891 there was a landmark legal case *Sharp v. Wakefield*, which established that a drinks licence could be revoked without compensation on the grounds that the licence was surplus to requirements. Previously revocations were dependent on misconduct charges being proven against the licensee. This case coincided with the expansion of the tied-house system which caused a significant rise in the value of pubs. Brewers became increasingly concerned that the value of their investments was being threatened by licensing committees, many of which had been infiltrated by temperance campaigners. Whilst Justices of the Peace who supported temperance were allowed to serve on licensing committees, JPs who were brewers were not. The bias of moral entrepreneurs was permissible, but that of commercial entrepreneurs was frowned on.

On the 18th March 1903 a drinks-trade delegation was sent to see the Conservative Prime Minister Arthur Balfour and his Home Secretary, CT Ritchie. They were sympathetic to the plea that over-zealous Justices presented an unjustified threat to their commercial interests. The outcome was the Licensing Act 1904, popularly known as the 'Balfour Act.' This Act introduced a compensation scheme which was funded by a levy on all licensed property, from £1 on small beer houses to £150 on large hotels (*Brewery History Journal 118, pp. 26-40*). This ensured that the owners of any pub that was closed down, for reasons other than misconduct, would be compensated with a sum of money equal to the difference in value of the premises with, and without a licence.

The hope was that this measure represented a compromise that would satisfy both brewers and temperance campaigners. The former because they would be compensated for loss of value, and the latter because it was estimated that between 2,000 and 2,500 redundant licences would be withdrawn every year. In the event it turned out to be a compromise that satisfied neither side. Brewers dubbed it the "Mutual Burial Fund" and temperance campaigners the "Brewers Endowment Fund." Meanwhile the Liberal opposition in Parliament accused the Tories of caving in to Trade pressure and vowed to take retaliatory measures when they were returned to power.

Their opportunity came when the general election of 1906 resulted in a landslide victory for the Liberals. The new Prime Minister Henry Campbell-Bannerman, and his Home Secretary Herbert Gladstone were called on by a delegation of 100 MPs demanding temperance measures. But it wasn't until the 27th February 1908 that the government made its plans clear. In a speech to the House of Commons, Chancellor of the Exchequer Herbert Asquith argued for the suppression of licences with the aim of closing a third of the public houses in England and Wales. The Licensing Bill also contained provisions for reducing Sunday opening hours and a ban on the employment of women in pubs.

Asquith's elevation to the position of Prime Minister, after Campbell-Bannerman's death on the 22nd April 1908, enabled him to argue passionately that these measures were needed to temper the nation's drinking habits. And this was a long-term plan that would see 30,000 of the nation's 96,000 pubs close over 14 years and nationalisation of the rest. Asquith was the UK's first lawyer Prime Minister. His legalistic reasoning was that the State 'owned' the liquor licences it granted and was therefore entitled to 'recover' them whenever it wanted. 90% of pub licences were tied to brewers and in his speech at the second reading of the Bill, Asquith had this to say: "The second great and governing purpose…is the recovery for the State of complete and unfettered control of this monopoly." He accused the brewers of inflating prices; producing poor quality, watered down beer; of "suicidal" competition to expand their tied estates *(Phil Mellows 'A Lesson from the Past, The Publican 15/12/08).*

Asquith was an unlikely champion of temperance, often observed swaying at the dispatch box, his name became synonymous with getting drunk – hence the term 'squiffy'! Unsurprisingly, these proposals horrified the Trade which mobilised on a scale not seen before or since. An early opportunity to test the public attitude to the Licensing Bill came with a by-election for the Liberal seat of Peckham in March, just before Campbell-Bannerman's death. Gooch, the Tory Party candidate, won the by-election after the appearance of paid orators and much public campaigning against the Licensing Bill made it a major issue. Over the following months the Liberals went on to lose eight more by-elections.

As in the 1855 protests, posters and leaflets played a major part in influencing public opinion on the issue. Although the Trade was fragmented with a plethora of local licensed victuallers' associations, local brewers and craft guilds, two umbrella organisations, the National Trade Defence Association and Allied Brewery Traders Association ensured a united front was presented in the face of this existential threat.

Posters and leaflets began to appear denouncing the Bill. It was variously described as 'un-English' and as advancing socialism. Moreover, it was claimed that its passage would raise the price of beer from tuppence halfpenny to fourpence a pint. The section in the Bill that proposed to outlaw the employment of barmaids also caused much consternation. Barmaids were heard to appeal to their customers to save their jobs and a petition of over 600,000 signatures was presented to the House of Commons.

The rationale for this section of the Bill (Section 20) is that it was immoral for women to be used to sell alcohol to working men, and that it might lead to the moral downfall of such women. The Bishop of Southwark, speaking in the House of Lords, commented: "The nation ought not to allow the natural attractions of a young girl to be used for trading purposes."

THE BARMAIDS POLITICAL DEFENCE LEAGUE

In response to Section 20 the suffragette Eva Gore-Booth and her lover Esther Roper formed the Barmaids Political Defence League. Apparently none of the country's estimated 100,000 barmaids ever joined the League; according to Gore-Booth they were much too busy! But its formation drew attention to the measure and it was withdrawn from the Bill before it reached the House of Lords.

THE HYDE PARK 'PEOPLE'S PROTEST' OF 27TH SEPTEMBER 1908

The campaign against the Bill led to mass meetings in Queen's Hall and the Albert Hall - the latter attended by Balfour, now leader of the opposition in Parliament. It culminated in a demonstration in Hyde Park that was organised by the National Trade Defence Association (NTDA - formed in 1888). On an overcast day the Association organised 166 trains to transport protesters from all over England and Wales. They arrived at London's major terminals and were met and marshalled by the NTDA, and organised behind banners that bore the name of the town or city of their origin.

1908 'People's Protest' against the licensing bill

There were over 500 banners, but none of them bore the name of a political organisation, such was the determination of the organisers to present this as a peoples' protest. Slogans such as "We oppose the Bill" and "Are we to be children again?" were the most common. Estimates of the size of this demonstration vary with 250,000 as the minimum, but according to the Brewery History Journal some 750,000 protesters turned up on the day. The demonstration was built up by countless local meetings and rallies in the weeks leading up to it and some 40 tons of campaign literature was distributed by the brewers, including 10 million leaflets, 409,000 posters and 780,000 cartoons that graphically warned of the impact the law would have on the working man's pint *(Phil Mellows: A lesson from the past, The Publican 15/12/08)*. Tickets for the trains were heavily subsidised too. In short, no stone was left unturned to ensure the size and success of the demonstration.

According to the Daily Graphic (28th September 1908) the slogans "Beer, beer, are we to part like this?" And the not-so-rhyming couplet "It's easy to be goody on other peoples' money" were also seen. Protesters wore badges which read "Honesty and Liberty", and some had sprigs of hops pinned to their chests.

The march was organised into 14 separate processions of which five were from London. The processions headed to the north of Hyde Park, accompanied by 100 brass bands and were then harangued from 20 platforms constructed around Reformer's Tree in a semicircle. At 4:30 p.m. the speeches against the Bill began from each platform and these were concluded with the sound of bugles at 5:15 p.m. The following resolution was read out from every platform:

"That this national demonstration protests against the provisions of the Licensing Bill on the grounds that it will fail to promote the cause of temperance, will violate those rights of property which have hitherto been encouraged and recognised by the State, will tend largely to the increase of unemployment, and will interfere with the reasonable liberty of the community." *(The Times 28/09/1908).*

According to The Times the resolution was carried with a "roar of cheering" and the crowd then began slowly to disperse. But not everyone went straight home. The Brewery History Society quotes the Westminster Gazette from the 28th September 1908: "Come evening, thousands of wearers, of all ages, of the 'honesty and liberty' button gave themselves up to liberty and license. They streamed through the West End and as far east as Fleet Street, storming the public houses on their way and frequently bursting into cheers and snatches of comic songs."

But the demonstrators' behaviour, while boisterous, was generally good humoured and well disciplined. The Brewing Trade Review of the 1st November 1908 quoted the Home Secretary as saying that arrests for drunkenness on the day of the demonstration were just 165, as compared to 144 arrests in the seven days prior to the demonstration.

THE DEFEAT OF THE LICENSING BILL

The attempt to pass the Licensing Bill of 1908 represented the high-water mark of the temperance movement. They had expanded their support beyond religious zealots and into the business community. The identification of Protestantism with the work ethic, and the concern that alcohol consumption was damaging industrial production, persuaded the Liberal government that something must be done.

The Bill made slow progress in the House of Commons, with over 1,000 amendments proposed. On the 20th November it passed its third reading by 350 votes to 113 and was sent to the Lords. It was in the Lords that it met with stiff opposition. Lord Lansdowne led the opposition in the Lords, despite being urged by Edward VII not to do so. He said: "The country looks to us to protect it from legislation which we believe to be iniquitous...We shall better deserve both the respect of our fellow countrymen and our own self-respect if straightforwardly and with the courage of our opinions we reject the Bill." On the 27th November it was defeated in the Lords by 272 votes to 96.

The Peel Commission report of 1896, which had inspired the Licensing Bill, declared that "the evils of the liquor traffic are a great bundle of sticks, more easily broken one by one." In trying to break them all at once Asquith succeeded in doing what no one has done before or since: he united a disparate drinks' industry that was riven with sectionalism and regionalism by confronting it with an existential threat that couldn't be ignored.

It is hardly surprising that such an assault on free enterprise and private property generated a response not just from the Trade, but from a House of Lords populated by hereditary peers whose wealth was based on land and property. They must have wondered who would be next should this measure pass unopposed. They didn't have to wait long to find out.

THE 'PEOPLE'S BUDGET' AND OTHER MEASURES

From the moment the Liberals won a landslide victory at the 1906 general election a clash between the elected House of Commons and the unelected House of Lords became more likely.

In the Commons the Liberals had 377 Members while the Conservatives had only 278; but in the Conservative-dominated Lords only 88 Members of the Lords out of 602 defined themselves as Liberals. With the new Government committed to a radical agenda of Irish home rule and social reform, it was likely the Upper House would seek to block certain pieces of legislation.

The Liberal MP David Lloyd George mocked Members of the Lords as "Five hundred men, accidently chosen from among the ranks of the unemployed." When a Conservative backbencher defended the Lords as the "watchdog of the constitution", Lloyd George quipped that it was in fact "Mr Balfour's poodle" (Arthur Balfour was Conservative leader in the Commons).

As the Parliament progressed the Lords was selective in which Bills it chose to block - the Education Bill of 1906 was the first, followed by the Licensing Bill of 1908 - while Campbell-Bannerman prepared plans for restricting the veto of Members of the Lords.

Matters came to a head in 1909 when the new prime minister Asquith and Lloyd George, the Chancellor, unveiled a radical Budget which proposed an increase in death, alcohol licensing and tobacco duties, a petrol tax, motor car licences and a differential rate of income tax on earned and unearned income. The most controversial provisions, however, were those for taxing large landowners, many of whom sat on the Conservative benches in the Commons and Lords.

Following bitter exchanges the Budget passed its third reading in the

Commons on the 25th November. Five days later it was rejected by the Lords. Although Members of the Lords were entitled to amend Money Bills, defeating a Budget went against parliamentary precedent.

This led to the introduction of the Parliament Act 1911 which restricted the power of the House of Lords to one of limited delay in respect of all public Bills and no right whatsoever to amend or delay Money Bills, including the Budget. It was intended to be a temporary measure pending a much more thoroughgoing constitutional reform in which the role of the Lords would be decided. More than 100 years later that is still to be decided and the Parliament Act 1911 is still the basis of the relationship between the two houses of the UK's Parliament.

In 1910 the Liberals also introduced the Licensing (Consolidation) Act which was a major licensing reform Act that repealed nearly all of the licensing laws of the past 80 years and codified them into a simpler form. Crucially for the Trade the new law did not attempt either wholesale closures or nationalisation of pubs. Perhaps that is the main achievement and lasting legacy of the Hyde Park demonstration of 1908.

THE CARLISLE EXPERIMENT

The advent of the First World War gave fresh impetus to the attempts to control the liquor trade. The Defence of the Realm Act, introduced in August 1914, gave new powers to military and naval authorities to close public houses and to restrict opening hours. These powers were extended to civil authorities shortly afterwards. In the UK, as in the United States, the justification was that alcohol drinking would jeopardise the war effort. In particular these concerns centred on war production in the munitions factories.

In October 1914 evening closing time in London was reduced from 12:30 a.m. to 10:00 p.m. In 1915 opening hours were reduced from 16-17 hours (19.5 in London) to 5.5 hours and evening closing was 9 – 9:30 p.m. (*Licensing – a Brief History, Camra, November 2003*). The Trade, in opposing these measures, could no longer rely on a Conservative majority in the House of Lords.

However, the most radical change came about in 1916 and came to be known as the 'Carlisle Experiment'. The government created the Central Control Board (Liquor Traffic), and the Board initially nationalised five breweries in Carlisle as well as 235 pubs in the Carlisle, Gretna and Annan area. In 1917 pubs in the Enfield Lock area of London and Invergordon in Scotland were taken over. In all, some 363 pubs were eventually nationalised over 300 square miles either side of the English-Scots border around Solway Firth, where a giant munitions factory was being built.

In all these areas the concern was that the efficiency of munitions production was undermined by drunkenness amongst the workers. The 'afternoon break' between 3:00 p.m. and 5:30 p.m. was also introduced at this time to ensure that workers didn't remain in the pub all afternoon! The State Management System, as it was called, also banned Sunday drinking, the consumption of spirits on a Saturday and the use of spirit-chasers.

The munitions factory at Gretna was the biggest in the world at that time. Its construction had a massive effect on nearby Carlisle where the population of some 52,000 was expanded by the arrival of 15,000 builders and munitions workers. With nothing to do but drink in the evening, the newcomers filled the pubs. From Prime Minister Lloyd George's point of view this created problems with absenteeism, hangovers and public disorder and it threatened the war effort.

The Central Control Board took an axe to licensing in the area, with 40% of all alcohol licences in the area being declared 'redundant', including all grocers' off-licences. External drinks advertising was banned, including hoardings and signs on the outside of pubs themselves – leaving nothing but a discreet sign giving the name of the pub.

Before Nationalisation

After Nationalisation

The Carlisle Experiment: WW1 Moral Panic

But it wasn't all bad. Owners and tenants were compensated and existing tenants offered jobs as managers of the pubs they had hitherto tenanted – with a fixed salary and 75% of the GP on food and other non-intoxicants. The rest of the profit accrued to the State. The Board also invested in pubs and built some new ones.

According to journalist Phil Mellows:

"Many backstreet boozers were closed down, but the Central Control Board also improved many remaining pubs to enable them to provide food and other alternatives to drink, and it created completely new pubs on an ideal model."

"A post office in Carlisle was converted into the Gretna Tavern (now the Gilded Lily) in July 1916. It comprised a bar and a separate 180 seat restaurant in the former sorting office. Food sales accounted for 66% of the total." *(The People's pubs, The Publican 22/06/09).*

THE LICENSING ACT 1921

Self-preservation is the iron law of bureaucracy, and so it is hardly surprising that after the war the Central Control Board recommended total nationalisation of the industry. Three different committees looked into it, but the cost was estimated at some £350 million at 1921 prices. The government eventually rejected full nationalisation, but continued with many of the wartime restrictions, such as the afternoon break and restricted Sunday opening. A minimum age of purchase for alcohol at 18 years, established in 1916, also remained in place as it has to this day.

The Licensing Act 1921 transferred all the pubs owned by the Central Control Board to the Home Office and the Scottish Office, but the State Management System, which was meant to be a temporary wartime measure, continued until 1971 when Conservative Prime Minister Edward Heath re-privatised all the pubs that remained in state ownership.

The licensing system established by the 1921 Act, and its subsequent amendments, remained in place until it was replaced by the Licensing Act 1964. The 1964 Act was eventually succeeded by the Licensing Act 2003, which commenced in November 2005. The 2003 Act was a major reform that swept away many of the outdated restrictions of the 1921 and 1964 licensing systems. The 2003 Act also re-activated the temperance movement, as we shall see in Part 3, Chapter 1: 'The Temperance Beast Awakes!'

Chapter 3:

Temperance Worldwide

—

In this chapter I examine some of the commonalities between UK and US Temperance and temperance movements in other countries, in terms of the influence of organised religion on the development of temperance sentiment.

The advent of temperance movements was not unique to Britain and the United States. Alcohol researchers have identified seven other temperance nations which saw similar developments. These are: Canada, Australia, New Zealand, Sweden, Iceland, Norway and Finland. All of these countries had significant teetotal or prohibitionist movements in the 19th century and they continue to harbour serious misgivings about alcohol consumption that are reflected in strict legal regulation. In Canada, for example, there is a State alcohol monopoly whereby the government is the sole importer of alcohol and in five out of Canada's seven provinces alcohol in the off-trade can be sold only from Government-owned liquor stores.

It is useful to examine what the UK has in common with these other temperance countries. Researcher Henry Yeoman cites two common explanations: that either industrialisation or high levels of consumption of spirits produce temperance movements, but, Yeoman asks, if this is correct why are other industrialised countries such as France and Germany non-temperance?

Similarly, the contention that drinking spirits - 'hard liquor' - produces an anti-alcohol reaction, fails to explain the fact that there is no temperance movement in Poland or the Czech Republic, whose populations both consume larger quantities of distilled spirits per head than any of the nine temperance cultures.

Religion, and in particular the strong historical presence of ascetic Protestantism in all nine temperance nations may be part of the explanation. This brand of Protestantism encompasses Calvinist-inspired denominations, such as Methodism, Baptism and Presbyterianism.

In the UK it is also evident that temperance groups were strongest in areas such as the South-West, the North and Scotland, where Non-conformism was rife, but weak in the South-East where the more Lutheran-influenced Church of England was dominant. Other researchers in this area support the idea that Calvinist-inspired religions are a causative factor. Joseph R. Gusfield describes how the American temperance movement drew a lot of its support from Calvinist congregations and, similarly, Harrison documents the overwhelmingly Calvinist make-up of the early teetotal movement in Britain. Eriksen describes the involvement of ascetic Protestants in starting the Swedish temperance movement.

French sociologist Emile Durkheim argued that Protestantism is more individualistic than Catholicism and substituted personal self-control for confessionary rituals. According to German sociologist Max Weber, this belief in self-control is further inflated by Calvinist strands of Protestantism.

Henry Yeoman further argues that "Calvinism thus intensifies the Protestant idea of self-control and places a powerful spiritual currency upon hard labour, financial thrift and other rational worldly activities. If alcohol costs money, disinhibits behaviour, inclines its drinkers towards spontaneity, and reduces capacity for work, it is apparent why such a thing would be morally anathema to Calvinists. It also becomes clear why more Lutheran countries, such as Germany or Denmark, did not witness large-scale temperance movements - their underlying religious ethics would not easily support this intensified reaction" *(Henry Yeoman, PH.d thesis,* 2009).

The classic puritanical view that pleasure is immoral arises from these ideas as recreation comes to be seen as a waste of time which could be used for rational labour, but also an act of revelling in the vulgarity of humanity and thus an affront to God. As drinking was, to a large extent, a recreational activity, it contravened acceptable Calvinist codes of behaviour. It starts to become clear why, to the Calvinist mind-set, total avoidance of alcohol was the only reasonable course of action.

I have discussed above the role of religion and religious value-systems as vehicles for temperance sentiment. Whilst it is obvious that alcohol is a product vulnerable to levels of misuse which contribute to problems such as crime and ill-health, what characterises temperance movements, and their various advocacy groups, is the scale of problem inflation they engage in with regard to alcohol's culpability for these problems. Absolutism is another feature of temperance beliefs - the first sip of alcohol transports the drinker to the top of a slippery slope. Negative health and social consequences of alcohol use came to be viewed as the typical and inevitable result of even modest consumption. Individuals lacking in self-discipline, able to resist anything except temptation were thus initiating their own descent into an uncontrollable, downward spiral of earthly sin and misery.

This pejorative definition of pleasure, in addition to the intensified ideas of rationality and self-control, were the basic ideological tenets which inclined ascetic Protestants against the use of alcohol. Driven by these anxieties about order and control, temperance campaigners were able to construct a causal inevitability which depicted any consumption of alcohol as physically and morally dangerous. If pleasure was theologically suspect and recreational drinking sure to be disastrous, alcohol use came to be constructed as a negative moral absolute.

Calvinist ideas thus provided a moral standpoint from which alcohol was viewed as evil. This new understanding instigated large-scale social movements against the use of alcohol in the UK and certain other countries in which ascetic Protestantism was strong. Despite this powerful ideological message and the movement's campaigning strength, religiously-inspired temperance in the UK, as a mass movement, had largely died out by the early 20th century. So, how was it possible that temperance ideas and beliefs were able to survive the demise of the social movement that spawned them?

ACHIEVING CULTURAL HEGEMONY: THE RISE AND DOMINANCE OF TEMPERANCE BELIEFS

Over the course of the 19th century, the moral crusade of the temperance movement became increasingly secularised. This mirrored the general historiography of a decline in church attendance and religious belief. I have argued how, in accordance with its Calvinist ideological ethos, the early temperance movement was very much the property of Non-conformist churches. But increasingly this social movement was adopted by Anglicans, and by the 1870s the Church of England Temperance Society had taken over much of the campaigning momentum.

Whilst it is true that temperance attitudes became more acceptable to Anglicans, temperance also began to lose its ties to institutional religion altogether. As we have seen, towards the end of the 19th century licensing became a major party political issue. Annual parliamentary votes on the Permissive Bill, which would have given local authorities a veto on the trade of alcohol in their local areas, reveal that from 1871 onwards the Liberal Party was more inclined toward temperance than the Conservatives. Many of those involved in the emerging Labour Party, such as Keir Hardie and

Sidney and Beatrice Webb, promoted temperance as a means to working-class self-improvement and this had also been reflected in the development of Temperance Chartism.

The temperance agenda thus became increasingly identifiable within parliamentary parties, and thus in the heart of secular government. The secularisation of the moral crusade enabled temperance ideas to migrate from the religious peripheries and settle in the political mainstream. But increasingly, and to this day, the role of moral entrepreneurs in promoting the moral viewpoint of temperance was taken up outside of Parliament by the medical profession. The torch of moral certainty still burned bright, but it passed from clerics to medics.

Part 2

From Clerics to Medics

—

'King Alcohol' 1880

Chapter 1:

Establishing Cultural Authority

—

This chapter discusses the process by means of which a social phenomenon becomes a social issue. Specifically, in relation to alcohol and its sale and consumption, I examine the role of moral entrepreneurs in establishing the conceptual and cultural frame of reference through which politicians, and the wider public, are invited to understand 'the issues'. It is a recurrent theme of this book that the 'alcohol problem' is socially constructed by those who have successfully established cultural authority over the issues, and are thereby able to represent the meanings they attach to these issues as constituting the consensus view.

I also examine how cultural ownership of the 'alcohol problem' has passed from clerics to medics; how the shift from religious to medico-scientific perspectives on alcohol has, nevertheless, failed to disguise the middle-class moral reform nature of the enterprise.

THE ROLE OF THE MORAL ENTREPRENEUR

I have argued that we cannot fully understand how and why temperance movements develop unless we place them into the context of longer term processes of moral regulation. If we are to develop this understanding we need to understand what 'moral regulation' means, and the role of 'moral entrepreneurs' in disseminating moral viewpoints and developing constituencies of support for them.

The role of moral entrepreneurs is abundantly apparent from reading the history of the alcohol issue. The term 'moral entrepreneur' is attributed to American sociologist Howard Saul Becker and refers to individuals, groups or organisations that seek to influence society, or groups of people in a society, to adopt or maintain a norm. In respect of individual moral entrepreneurs: these are people who take the lead in labelling the behaviour of others in a variety of ways, both positive and negative. Social labelling is therefore instrumental in creating social norms and in defining what constitutes deviance from those norms.

Becker defines two categories of moral entrepreneur: *rule creators and rule enforcers*. If we apply this concept to the history of temperance and prohibition in America and the UK we can see some very prominent examples of both types. Frances E. Willard, second President of the WCTU, is very definitely a rule creator; a moraliser who sought not only to live her own life according to a set of moral rules, but to write moral prescriptions for others. Her WCTU colleague Mary Hanchet Hunt, who founded the Department of Scientific Temperance Instruction in Schools and Colleges, clearly falls into the rule enforcer category. And without a doubt Carry A. Nation's campaign of 'hatchetation' dramatically illustrates that she also falls within the rule enforcer category.

Currently in the UK we see a variety of individuals and advocacy groups that play the role of moral entrepreneur in relation to the current moral panic over alcohol use; Professor Sir Ian Gilmore, who leads the Alcohol Health Alliance, is an individual moral entrepreneur; and temperance advocacy group Alcohol Concern is an example of an organisational moral entrepreneur.

Moral entrepreneurs are instrumental in establishing cultural ownership of a moral, social or political issue and they usually represent a cultural viewpoint, class interest or other interest group. Successful moral crusades are generally dominated by those in the upper strata of society. In both America and the UK moral entrepreneurs are invariably middle class; their crusades frequently reactionary in the literal sense of the word – a reaction to a challenge to the cultural hegemony of the class or interest group they represent.

The middle-class nature of moral crusades reflects the fact that only the middle class and above occupy positions in the social strata that give them access to ideas, education and the time to reflect on the conditions in society. And the access that the middle class has to the political class and to the media empowers them to create moral panics.

A social issue emerges as a social problem because moral entrepreneurs construct campaigns in which they name, interpret and dramatize the issues by inculcating rhetorical typologies that invite the public to frame those issues in a particular way. In the case of the alcohol issue the language employed has assisted in moving cultural ownership from clerics to medics. The language, imagery and characterisation of the alcohol issue in the UK today is dominated by middle-class moral-entrepreneurs who invite the public and the political class to view alcohol use almost exclusively through the paradigm of 'problem drinking.'

The success of moral entrepreneurs in de-normalising drinking rests on their ability to identify entire groups of drinkers as deviant. 'Binge drinkers', 'chronic drinkers', 'underage drinkers' and delinquent 'pre-loaders' are all characterised as behaving in ways that are morally, medically and socially dangerous and thus constitute a threat to themselves and the rest of society.

ESTABLISHING CULTURAL OWNERSHIP OF THE ALCOHOL ISSUE

As we have seen, historically, the 'alcohol issue' has frequently demonstrated its capacity to mediate wider social anxieties. The struggle in the United States for temperance, and later for the outright legal prohibition of alcohol, exemplifies how establishing cultural ownership of a social issue enables those who do so to present their moral view as the consensus view. Where a contest of meanings over a social issue takes place between one group and another, in a given society, this can have a meaning that goes beyond the specifics of the issue itself, and can come to symbolise where one group stands in relation to the other in that society's status hierarchy. To put it another way: once an adversarial issue becomes constructed in moral terms, it becomes a status conflict in which what is at stake is the status of each interest group as 'rule creators', or 'value givers' in that society.

As I have argued in Part I, Chapter I, in 19th and early 20th century America support for temperance, abstinence and the legal prohibition of alcohol was strongest amongst the Protestant, rural, 'nativist' middle class – the well-established descendants of the original colonists. Their adherence to ascetic brands of Calvinist-inspired Protestantism provided the cultural and religious basis of an ideology that valued individual responsibility, self-control and abstemious lifestyles. This group felt challenged and threatened by the influx of new immigrants from countries with hard-drinking traditions, such as those of Germany and Ireland, whose Catholic religious beliefs centred on confessionary rituals of sin and repentance. The fact that these immigrants settled mostly in the burgeoning towns and cities of an America that was fast industrialising, only served to dramatize the cultural divide.

The struggle between these two groups can be characterised as an interest-group status-conflict to establish who would be the value-givers of American society.

Today, in the UK, I would argue that we are witnessing a similar symbolic moral crusade over alcohol. It is complex, multi-layered, and has created some unlikely political alliances. From the 1950s onwards there has been a fault-line running through our society between the cultural fundamentalism of the old, established middle class of the shires, and the social liberalism of a post-war generation that wanted to throw off outdated social mores, and whose middle class is primarily located in the metropolitan urban centres.

Over the past 60 years the cultural polarities of our national life have been deeply influenced by new, cosmopolitan ideas that have reached us via a global movie industry, televisual media, including satellite TV, the internet and the affordability of international travel. New fashions and lifestyles that have challenged the parochialism of the old, established middle class have resulted in a split that has divided it, and divided the wider society, into two main cultural groups. One group reasserts older, traditional values which have their genesis in the 'producer culture' of the 19th century. The other group identifies 'the modern' as the normative social order to be followed and associates this with 'consumer culture'. The new middle class looks outward and for them change is identified with progress and is welcomed. The cultural fundamentalists of the old middle class look inward. For them change is troubling, disruptive and threatening. Here we have the classic ingredients of an interest-group status-conflict - whose values will prevail?

On all the major cultural issues of the past 50 years – sexual freedom, divorce, abortion, capital punishment, censorship – the status of the old, established middle class has been diminished by the successful challenge of a new middle class of salaried professionals, employed managers and skilled workers, as well as the development of an economically enfranchised youth culture. But in relation to alcohol the cultural fundamentalists have held the line. That is, until the advent of the Licensing Act 2003 and its portrayal as a 'liberalising Act' that would deregulate alcohol sales and facilitate '24-hour drinking.' This presented a threat and a challenge to the moral hegemony of the cultural fundamentalists who felt obliged to defend one of their few remaining redoubts. Since then we have seen a relentless attack on the licensed retail sector, the partying culture of the city-centre night-time economy, and the creation of the 'binge drinker' as a new and dangerous devil has been added to the pantheon of social demons that frighten middle England.

We can see this moral panic being played out in our national press. The Daily Mail is the newspaper of the cultural fundamentalist, fierce in its defence of old middle-class values. Its ritual denunciation of the permissiveness of the 'metropolitan liberal elite' is an expression of protest against the diminishing status of those who espouse self-restraint and abstemious lifestyles. And it is the Daily Mail that has led the charge against the perceived liberalisation of the Licensing Act 2003.

So, on one level the current 'alcohol issue' can be characterised as a status conflict between the old and the new middle-class. But this does not fully explain the role of the public health lobby in the whole controversy. Historically, the values of abstinence and temperance were espoused by clergy. But in our increasingly secular society this role has been usurped by public health professionals and doctors - the secular priests of our time. So whilst we have seen a divide between the cultural fundamentalism of the old middle-class and the more liberal inclinations of the new one, we have at the same time seen the exponential development of a welfare state that underpins middle-class lifestyles, and protects the middle class from being thrust down into poverty. Public health professionals are, at one and the same time, natural exponents of the traditional middle class values of self-restraint and individual responsibility – 'sensible drinking', 'healthy eating choices', 'five a day' etc., but additionally have a new, and vast set of vested interests of their own to defend.

With NHS spending just south of £110 billion annually, there is great pressure to defend the service by locating existential cost threats that are external to its structure. This effort is aided by the relentless problem-inflation of Alcohol Concern and other neo-prohibitionist groups.

So we have an unusual confluence of political views: on the one hand cultural fundamentalists, for whom the battle over alcohol is a symbolic moral crusade by means of which they hope to resurrect their status as the 'value-givers' of our society; and on the other hand, activist health professionals, and other public sector workers, piously occupying blameless niches, detached from the world of production and trade, who strive to elevate public health to the level of a societal value that trumps all other considerations. If the Daily Mail and columnists like Peter Hitchens represent a nostalgic desire to return to a rose-tinted vision of a perfect Britain that never-was; the Guardian and columnists like Polly Toynbee articulate the opinions of an effete group of smug public sector critics of profit who are nevertheless happy to live off the taxes created by those who make it.

The moral certainties of both groups create a dilemma for democratic politicians. As a 'broker of interests' the democratic politician instinctively handles all political issues as matters of bargaining. He seeks to adjust one set of interests and values to another, in order to split the difference and produce a compromise acceptable to both sides. For the moraliser in politics compromise is anathema – tantamount to a sell-out. For him, political issues are tests of virtue and vice in which those on the opposite side are immoral.

This is the reason why opinion on the alcohol issue is now more polarised than ever. It also explains why much of the Coalition Government's Alcohol Strategy (2012) reads as if it comes straight from the Daily Mail playlist, which abhors alcohol and links it with public disorder and 'yobbishness'; and it also echoes the Guardian narrative of opposition to an alcohol industry that it identifies as putting profit ahead of public health. The Alcohol Strategy's outline and prescriptions caricature the licensed retail sector by insisting that we view it through the lens provided by tabloid TV and red-top newspapers. Our mass media create a false consciousness by holding up a distorting mirror that presents the worst excesses of the night-time economy, and invites us to conclude that the untypical is in fact all-too-typical. The Alcohol Strategy panders to this lowest common denominator of media-induced public prejudice. The real purpose of it is to appeal politically to the cultural fundamentalism of the old middle-class of the shires - the core of Conservative Party support. In short, control of alcohol has become a dog-whistle party-political issue.

We are living through a time of unprecedented economic crisis. The consumption bubble has burst and we are exhorted to re-balance our economy away from consumerism towards production. If this is to become a long-term trend it will require a major adjustment to our value system as a society. It's not difficult to see how the need to promote belt-tightening and austerity chimes with the call for temperance and responsible drinking. Value systems are cultural superstructures that rest on economic sub-structures.

MORAL PANICS AND HISTORICAL PROCESSES

I have discussed the role of moral entrepreneurs in establishing cultural ownership of moral and social issues and their role in facilitating moral panics that bring these issues to the attention of the public and the political class. As described in the Introduction to this book, 'moral panics' can be characterised as official reactions to certain social phenomenon that are entirely disproportionate to the actual level of threat posed. In Stanley Cohen's famous definition, "A condition, person or group of people comes to be viewed as a threat to societal values and interests with the result that the moral barricades are manned by editors, bishops, politicians and other right thinking people." This noisy reaction by establishment figures draws public attention to the issue and wider condemnation often ensues.

The end result of this panic, according to Cohen, is that "ways of coping are evolved or (more often) resorted to" and consequently "the condition disappears, submerges or deteriorates and becomes more visible."

This traditional conception of moral panic has been the subject of some criticism and debate. Since Culture Wars and Moral Panic is the title of this book, I think it is appropriate to provide a brief explanation of why I think the use of the term 'moral panic' is justified when referring to the recurrent episodes of heightened public alarm over alcohol.

Cohen's inference that episodes of moral panic are exceptional rather than routine presupposes that there is some kind of natural social equilibrium that is occasionally upset when people perceive some new threat. This position has been contested. For example it is argued that in the Victorian era, and today, episodes of moral panic were and are frequent. Hence, some prefer the term 'social panic' which reflects the current state of ongoing rather than exceptional cases of alarmist public discourse.

With reference to attitudes to alcohol, this less-disjointed approach seems more suitable as alcohol has proved a recurrent theme in public discourse. The idea that public anxiety about alcohol is temporary is thus questionable. However, I do myself believe that the concept of moral panic is a viable explanatory model that aids understanding of the alcohol issue. Although there are on-going concerns about alcohol use, there are nevertheless identifiable periods of time when that concern spikes and public and political anxiety becomes heightened and moves to the top of the political agenda. The long period between the two world wars, and subsequent to them, during which alcohol sales in the UK were subject to a licensing system that was comprehensive and restrictive, was a period during which public and political concern about alcohol was relatively low-key. It was also a period in which the old-established middle class of the shires were unquestionably the value-givers for British society, or at least for 'public morality.' It is only when their cultural hegemony was challenged that alcohol again moved to the top of the agenda.

The theoretical frameworks that I've used in this book to make sense of temperance and prohibition are primarily 'moral-panic theory' and 'interest-group status-conflict theory.' I think that if social science can't discern a social reality that is independent of subjective perception then it has little point. A social scientific theory must do one of two things: provide a predictive model for the future or an explanatory model of the past. Analysing the historical discourse contained in this book, including the recent history described in Part 3, within the framework of the sociological theories identified above, has therefore provided me with a conceptual framework within which to uncover a social reality that would otherwise not be apparent from a mere factual narrative of historical events and turning points.

Chapter 2:

The Disease Theory of Alcoholism and Public Health Perspectives

—

In this chapter I provide an historical discourse analysis of the early development of mainstream alcohol science in the US and discuss the disease theory of alcoholism as one paradigm through which we have been invited to view the 'alcohol problem.'

I contrast the disease theory with contemporary public health approaches to dealing with the alcohol issue.

Medical Temperance and its various advocacy groups invite us to see alcohol use through the twin paradigms of 'problem drinking' and 'chronic drinking', or 'alcoholism' as it is more popularly known. The 'medicalisation' of certain drinking patterns has created a perception of them as a disease, an illness, rather than as a personal moral failing or as a reaction to the stresses and strains of the social conditions that surround the drinker. This 'disease theory of alcoholism' is just that – a theory – but the term 'alcoholism' is one of those words, like 'psychopath' or 'paranoid', that started off having a quite limited meaning for medical practitioners, but has now found its way into the lexicon of general parlance.

In this section I want to critically examine the proposition that chronic and damaging use of alcohol is a disease, an addictive illness.

THE DISEASE THEORY OF ALCOHOLISM

According to Dr. Herbert Fingarette the disease theory of alcoholism is based on four propositions:

1. Heavy problem-drinkers show a single distinctive pattern of ever greater alcohol use leading to ever greater bodily, mental, and social deterioration.

2. The condition, once it appears, persists involuntarily: the craving is irresistible and the drinking is uncontrollable once it has begun.

3. Medical expertise is needed to understand and relieve the condition ('cure the disease') or at least ameliorate its symptoms.

4. Alcoholics are no more responsible legally or morally for their drinking and its consequences than epileptics are responsible for the consequences of their movements during seizures.

(Herbert Fingarette, Why we should reject the disease theory of alcoholism, Controversies in the Addictions Field).

There has been speculation about alcoholism as a disease at least since the American physician Dr Benjamin Rush published his Inquiry into the Effects of Ardent Spirits upon the Human Body and Mind, and its Influence upon the Happiness of Society in 1785. However, the main proponent of the modern disease theory was E.M. Jellinek who began writing and theorising about it in the 1940s.

The proposition that heavy problematic use of alcohol could only amplify into ever-greater use leading to progressive physical, mental and social deterioration was given credibility by Jellinek's study of the 'phases of alcoholism' in 1946. Jellinek's study represented a growing trend towards the medicalization of moral propositions. As we have seen, the 19th century temperance movement portrayed even the mild use of alcohol as transporting the drinker to the top of a slippery slope leading to ever-greater use and moral and physical decline.

Jellinek simply wrapped this moral proposition in the white coat of science from which it gained credibility.

Jellinek's hypothesis was based on questionnaires that were prepared and distributed by Alcoholics Anonymous and completed by the recipients. There were less than 100 questionnaires completed, all by men, and the results were analysed by Jellinek. To be fair to him, Jellinek was not a pseudo-scientist, despite doubts being raised with regard to the authenticity of his doctorate, and he recognised the scientific inadequacy of a survey of less than 100 handpicked male alcoholics. He saw this merely as a starting point that justified the need for further research. But it was seized on by others and soon came to be accepted as scientific fact in much the same way as the recent Sheffield Alcohol Pricing Model (SAPM) has been similarly misrepresented.

However, subsequent research has demonstrated that the typical pattern of heavy drinking fluctuates. There isn't a pre-ordained, chemically driven inevitability about what came to be called 'Jellinek's curve', whereby there was a one-way movement down the slippery slope. Some drinkers get worse, some improve, some don't change and yet others develop different problems from the ones Jellinek identified (Problem Drinking Among American Men, Cahalan and Room 1974).

As researchers Joseph R. Gusfield and Stanton Peele have shown, the second proposition is disproved by the fact that some alcoholics return to controlled or moderate drinking. The third proposition, that medical intervention is needed to 'cure' the disease of alcoholism is also demonstrably untrue. Most alcoholics, like most heroin addicts, control or modify their behaviour without the need for outside intervention. Indeed, recovery rates for alcoholics using the Alcoholics Anonymous 12-step approach are lower than those of 'self-cured' alcoholics.

The fourth proposition, that alcoholism is a kind of chemical enslavement that excuses the individual from any moral or social responsibility for their own condition now seems hopelessly simplistic and dated.

THE POST-REPEAL HISTORY OF ALCOHOL SCIENCE

In trying to understand how the disease theory of alcoholism came about we need to appreciate how the mainstream scientific understanding of alcohol use evolved in the early years after the repeal of American Prohibition in 1933.

Post-repeal there was no mainstream alcohol-science research endeavour in the United States and it was common to perceive alcoholism as a moral failing. The medical profession of the time treated it as incurable and likely to lead to death. Such medical treatment as was available was based on the administration of Barbiturate and Belladonna; this 'treatment' was known as 'purge and puke'. In 1935 Alcoholics Anonymous (AA) was founded by Bill Wilson and Dr. Robert Smith. The treatment programmes later developed by AA – the 12-step programme – and others, were not really medical programmes but programmes that attempted to give the alcoholic a spiritual release from the enslavement of alcohol dependence.

In trying to understand how a new, mainstream alcohol science came about we have to recognise the context in which alcohol science, and scientific endeavour generally, was viewed by the American public in the 1930s. The landscape must have looked particularly bleak to alcohol scientists in post-repeal America. The pseudo-science of Mary Hanchett-Hunt and the WCTU's Department of Scientific Temperance Instruction in Schools and Colleges had been repudiated by the Committee of Fifty some 30 years earlier. During the Prohibition era there had been claim and counter-claim about the effects of alcohol from both sides of the debate, most of which didn't deserve to be dignified by referring to them as 'scientific'. The public of recession-hit America did, to some extent, blame scientific and technological advance for throwing hard-working Americans out of their jobs and so the perception of the scientific community was that science had to find a way of justifying itself as socially useful. In fact the American Association for the Advancement of Science saw it as a core part of its mission to provide such justifications.

An alcohol science that addressed the problems of society's choices in relation to alcohol in post-repeal America therefore came along at the right time, but faced a number of dilemmas. What would a new alcohol science contribute to understanding and how would this new understanding benefit society? What research problems would it tackle? For a scientific community searching for social relevance the temptation to view alcohol abuse as symptomatic of a previously unidentified disease was both tempting and convenient. E.M. Jellinek was crucial to the development of this new, mainstream alcohol science, although he was not the originator of it.

E.M. Jellinek

E.M. JELLINEK

Elvin Morton Jellinek (1890 – 1963) was born in New York City and was the son of Hungarian-Jewish immigrants. There is very little known of his early life or of his college career, but subsequent to it he served for a short period of time as a captain in the Hungarian Red Cross in WWI, where he was involved in carrying medical supplies to the front line. After Hungary's defeat he worked briefly in a government school for 'nervous children' and then became involved in currency speculation. According to his daughter, Ruth Surry, he went bankrupt in 1920, taking others down with him, and then disappeared.

Some five years later he made fresh contact with his family and was working under an assumed name, 'Nikita Hartman', for a steamship company that operated out of Sierra Leone. Later in the 1920s, still under the Hartman name, Jellinek worked in the Honduras for the United Fruit Company on banana research.

By some accounts Jellinek was a bit of a charlatan. He appears to have fabricated his doctorate and may not have a held any college degree at all. Early papers that he published in the Quarterly Journal of Studies on Alcohol indicated that his doctorate was 'honorary', but in later papers the 'honorary' descriptor was dropped. Notwithstanding this, he was stoutly defended by his research colleagues and his contribution to the newly developing alcohol science of the time was considerable, although not necessarily as a result of scientific endeavour.

In 1931 he took a job as a biostatistician at the Worcester State Hospital in Massachusetts and from there he entered the field of alcohol research in 1939 at the age of 50, when he was hired by Dr. Norman Jolliffe to manage the new Carnegie Project. This project was the first substantial research grant to be won by a group called the Research Council on Problems of Alcohol, from which a new, mainstream alcohol science was emerging. It appears that at this point Jellinek knew little about alcohol research, and according to his daughter "knew little about alcoholism, but was interested so he got some books on the subject and spent a weekend in bed studying" *(Ron Roizen, E.M. Jellinek and All That)*. Clearly he knew when he was on to a good thing because he devoted the rest of his life to the subject and became a hero for the emerging alcohol science movement.

Jellinek's two most important scientific contributions were the description of the 'alcoholism syndrome' and an 'alcoholism prevalence' formula that bore his name and was based on contemporary cirrhosis mortality statistics. The Jellinek formula is a method for estimating the prevalence of alcoholism from liver cirrhosis mortality data. Its underlying rationale is quite simple: the formula asks how big must the pool of living alcoholics be in order to provide a certain number of cirrhosis deaths among alcoholics in a given year? It begs the question: what do we mean by an 'alcoholic'?

This definitional problem illustrates just one of the difficulties experienced by the emerging alcohol science. When the formula was first being worked out the word 'alcoholic' had a rather different meaning for Jellinek from the meaning it later acquired. In the early 1940s the term 'alcoholic' referred to a person with a physical illness related to his drinking. Thus, for example, an 'alcohol addict' was not necessarily an 'alcoholic' unless he or she also manifested some alcohol-related physical illness. Also, someone who was not dependent on alcohol, but nevertheless had acquired a physical illness related to drinking would qualify as an alcoholic. The original Jellinek formula was calculated with this definition of alcoholism in mind.

By the late 1940s and early 1950s the term 'alcoholism' had taken on a broader meaning for Jellinek: it came to include persons who did not necessarily have an alcohol-related physical illness. Thus, it was necessary for the calculation of the old formula to be increased by a factor that expressed the ratio of all alcoholics (whether or not they had a physical illness) to alcoholics with a physical illness. In the new nomenclature this was termed the ratio of "alcoholics with and without complications" to "alcoholics with complications." The term 'alcoholic with complications' then took on the meaning the term 'alcoholism' alone had in the early 1940s. It is not difficult to see how this early example of problem-inflation was beneficial to the future of the emergent alcohol science. There's nothing like identifying a problem that is apparently growing dramatically to justify ongoing research and research grants.

Both of Jellinek's main scientific papers were published in the early 1950s, and they related to the description of the 'alcoholism syndrome' and the 'alcoholism prevalence formula' that bore his name. The first of these was as a research note in the Quarterly Journal for the Study of Alcoholism (QJSA) and the second as an annex to a World Health Organisation (WHO) report. His main contribution to alcohol science was in the 1940s as the man who publicised and popularised the whole endeavour. He articulated America's long-standing and deep-seated anxieties about alcohol and mapped-out the role of science in defining the relationship between alcohol and society.

E.M. Jellinek died of a heart attack at Stanford in 1963 at the age of 73.

THE CARNEGIE PROJECT

Creating a disease theory of alcoholism took the issue away from clerics and gave it to medics. For a nation that had just repealed Prohibition and that had historically viewed alcoholism as a personal moral failing, albeit one that was induced by a wicked folk devil called 'Big Alcohol' that placed temptation in the path of the weak and morally disabled, this notion came as a great relief. If it was an illness, a disease that afflicted a discrete group of people, then it could safely be left to the doctors and the heat could go out of the politics that had previously been attached to it.

The Carnegie Project was the first major grant to finance the new, mainstream alcohol research. Knowledge about the Carnegie Project is somewhat sketchy. Much of it comes from Mark Keller (*History of the Alcohol Problems Field The Drinking and Drug Practices Surveyor 14:22-28, 1979*) who worked as Dr. Norman Jolliffe's editorial and research assistant at Bellevue Hospital, New York. According to Keller, Jolliffe, who was a Bellevue internist and faculty member of the NYU Medical School, had applied to the Rockefeller foundation for a seven-year grant to study alcoholism. He was in a good position to do so as he had access to the steady flow of admissions to Bellevue's alcoholism ward, so had plenty of subjects to base his research on.

However, the Rockefeller establishment's early interest in this project flagged after they had sent Jolliffe on a European tour of alcoholism treatment and research projects. NYU then organised a high-powered scientific advisory committee to give gravitas to Jolliffe's putative project. This advisory committee in due course became the Research Council on Problems of Alcohol (RCPA).

The RCPA sought the approval of the American Association for the Advancement of Science, and that was duly forthcoming because of the aforementioned concern about the role that science and labour-saving technological devices was perceived to have played in the growth of unemployment. A mainstream alcohol-research science that could demonstrate its social relevance therefore suited modern scientific endeavour generally, and not just those concerned with the relationship between alcohol and society.

BOOK-BURNING – TEMPERANCE STRIKES BACK!
But not everyone was happy with the new alcohol science endeavour. The temperance movement believed that it was totally unnecessary to prove the dangers of alcohol scientifically – after all, hadn't they done so already? A dramatic confrontation took place in the spring of 1938 between temperance sentiment and mainstream scientific evaluations of alcohol. In Virginia, two pharmacology professors, J.A. Waddell and H.B. Haag, had produced an overview report on alcohol's effects on the human organism at the request of the state's legislature, which hoped the new review would reconstitute the state's alcohol pedagogy.

When news leaked that the review suggested that the moderate consumption of alcohol was not harmful, temperance organisations were stirred to action and deluged the legislature and the Governor's office with objections. Such was the residual power of the temperance movement, even five years after the repeal of Prohibition, that the state legislature voted for all 1,000 copies of Waddell and Haag's report to be burned – unread! The burning was duly carried out in the capitol's furnace by the building's fire marshal on the 26th April 1938.

If this was meant to deter the members of the RCPA it had the opposite effect. The text of the RCPA's proposal for the Carnegie grant, written a year later, referred directly to the book-burning in Virginia: "In consideration of this experience and of the confused state of public opinion regarding the effects of alcohol, it seems especially desirable that a further fact-finding be conducted by a large and representative group of scientists of unquestioned authority." *(Ron Roizen, The American Discovery of Alcoholism, 1933-1939, Ph.D dissertation, Sociology, University of California, Berkeley, 1991).*

Whilst, in Ron Roizen's words "the Council saw itself as a kind of scientific cavalry, riding in to give Waddell and Haag's beleaguered scientific outpost much needed back-up", from the perspective of understanding the bigger picture, this background explains why such a high-powered scientific assemblage was needed to get the new Council off to a good start. Both Repeal and the Great Depression formed the backdrop that shaped the new alcohol science endeavour.

Jellinek's discovery of 'alcoholism' as a new disease thus provided a *modus vivendi* between the old temperance movement and the new science of alcohol, and created a cultural niche in which such an endeavour might flourish, and provide much needed employment for research scientists whilst offering some measure of redemption for science generally in the eyes of society.

CULTURAL OWNERSHIP AND CONSENSUS

It is a recurrent theme of this book that when moral entrepreneurs gain cultural ownership of an issue they are able to represent their view of the issue as the consensus view. Mainstream alcohol-science morphed into medical temperance because its need to demonstrate social relevance created a particular dynamic. Put simply, alcohol scientists needed something to hang their hat on. The disease theory of alcoholism provided the peg. A collation of public surveys conducted in the period between 1946 and 1951 indicated that a growing number of people thought of alcoholism as a disease. About 20% of the general population of the US thought that alcoholism was a disease in 1946 to 1950. About 60% thought so in 1955-1960, and by the early 1960s the percentage agreeing with this view had risen to 65% *(Stanton Peele, The Meaning of Addiction, p.28)*. As Robin Room went on to point out, those who endorsed the 'disease position' also simultaneously held on to the view that the alcoholic was, nevertheless, morally deficient.

So, by the mid-1960s mainstream alcohol science had succeeded in effecting a hugely significant transformation of public and medical attitudes: that alcoholism was a disease and that medical treatment was the appropriate response to that disease. At the same time, the disease theory of alcoholism was inclusive enough to accommodate those whose moralism caused them to oppose alcohol use. One of the key parts of the disease theory of alcoholism is the alcoholic's loss of control; the proposition that the inability to drink moderately leads to the habit only to drink to intoxication. According to the theory only the true 'gamma alcoholic' manifests this inability, whereas some who get drunk do so as a matter of choice. At the same time alcoholism is presented as a progressive disease, meaning that from the early symptoms to gamma alcoholism there is an inevitable and inexorable progression. This was the conclusion reached by Jellinek as a result of his study of 98 members of Alcoholics Anonymous.

However, virtually every independent attempt to test Jellinek's typology of alcoholism found that it doesn't follow any particular path of development and that there is no internal mechanism that accounts for the alcoholic's loss of control, nor could this be put down to the absence of such a mechanism. On the contrary, researchers have shown that alcoholics with every degree of severity of the problem can recover without treatment and return to non-problematic drinking. And laboratory studies have shown that alcoholics typically do regulate their drinking *(Mello and Mendelson, 1971)*.

The transition of the alcohol issue from clerics to medics was further aided by the contemporaneous development of Alcoholics Anonymous *(AA)*. AA accepted that alcoholism was a disease and shared with temperance the view that complete, lifelong abstinence was necessary. Thus, in the tortuous language presently applied: an alcoholic is never 'cured', he or she is persuaded to regard themselves as inhabiting the permanent limbo of the 'recovering alcoholic', always at risk of falling off the wagon, such is the power of the chemical grip exerted by the demon drink.

AA meetings had other commonalities with 19th century temperance. A typical AA meeting is like a Protestant revivalist meeting: people come together in an emotionally charged atmosphere and stand up and relate their struggle with alcohol; they receive the (often rapturous) support of their peers and allegedly gain strength from the apparent solidarity in much the same way that religious revivalist meetings involve people standing up to confess their sins, express contrition and a willingness to submit themselves to the will of God in order to gain salvation. So, AA bridged the gap between temperance notions of alcoholism as a sin and the medical science voodoo of the disease theory of alcoholism. Abstinence as an essential part of the 'cure' for alcoholism is therefore rooted culturally and emotionally, not empirically.

Chapter 3:

Chapter 3: The Sociological Challenge to Public Health Orthodoxy

———

In this chapter I discuss how a social constructionist approach to understanding alcohol use might provide the means by which to challenge the cultural hegemony of medical temperance and neo-prohibitionism.

I analyse how the examination of alcohol use through the twin paradigms of 'problem drinking' and 'pathological drinking' have obscured the positive social meanings of alcohol use. I re-examine where the problems of alcohol use might actually be located, and how to tackle them. I place contemporary alcohol use in the context of historical social ritual and changes to the way in which we divide work and leisure.

Although the disease theory of alcoholism in its original form has been superseded by modern concepts of addiction, the public health approach to reducing alcohol-related harms still essentially accepts that among the harms to be prevented is 'alcoholism', which comprises the illnesses brought on by excessive alcohol consumption and the addictive nature of the substance of alcohol itself. These two elements – alcohol-related medical conditions and substance addiction – were the basis of Jellinek's revised concept of alcoholism that I described in *Chapter 2: The Disease Theory of Alcoholism and Public Health Perspectives.*

In the first part of this chapter I want to critically examine the proposition that alcohol is an addictive substance and to contrast a social constructionist approach to the understanding of alcohol use and alcohol problems.

DOES ALCOHOL CAUSE ALCOHOLISM?

The notion of 'addictive substances' is one with a long history. The implication is that addiction is a kind of chemical enslavement that results from the exposure of the brain to the substance and its frequent or habitual use. In relation to alcohol, the fact that most people use alcohol in a controlled way is explained away by adherents of the 'addictive substance' theory by suggesting that alcoholism is a continuum. This enables them to neatly get over a number of definitional problems, such as when exactly does alcohol use morph into 'alcoholism'? A subtle change in the language is employed to blur the edges. 'Addiction' as a descriptor is replaced by 'dependence'. On the basis of this narrative anyone who regularly drinks alcohol is exhibiting 'dependence', all that differs is the degree of dependence and the extent to which it has come to predominate and negatively affect the social and psychological functioning of the individual concerned.

This proposition represents little more than the co-option by medical temperance of the old moral temperance idea of the 'slippery slope.' Go on any internet site that claims to help you determine whether or not you have an 'alcohol problem' and you will invariably find that you are asked questions like: "Have you ever got home after a hard day at work and thought 'I could murder a cold beer'?" The suggestion is that you should re-define normal drinking behaviour and the commonplace desire for refreshment and a change of mood as symptomatic of an incipient dependence problem. Thus the scene is set for pathologising and de-normalising drinking behaviour.

Whereas the 1940's version of the disease theory of alcoholism conjured up by the Yale University Center of Alcohol Studies (whose main advocates were Jellinek and Keller) suggested that only a small group of habitual drunks got the 'disease', the 19th century temperance version of alcoholism focussed on the substance itself, claiming that the disease befell anyone who drank regularly and who frequently got drunk. It seems that the disease theory of alcoholism has come full circle: modern notions of alcoholism see it as just the extreme end of a spectrum of dependence. Those who arrive at the bottom of this slippery slope are characterised as having a brain chemistry that exhibits a peculiar sensitivity or allergy to alcohol that leads to uncontrollable cravings, or, alternatively, perhaps they are genetically pre-disposed to alcoholism.

MODELS OF ADDICTION

Addiction, in its classical formulation, is defined by three factors: tolerance, withdrawal and craving. A person addicted to a substance can be recognised by his intensified and chronic need to imbibe or use; by intense physical and mental suffering which results if he can't use for any length of time (withdrawal symptoms); and by that person's willingness to go to great lengths to satisfy his craving. These signs of addiction, which are not restricted to alcohol, have all been observed, but as addiction expert Stanton Peele points out: "the inadequacy of this conventional understanding lies not in the observations, but in the processes that are imagined to account for them" *(Stanton Peele, The Meaning of Addiction).*

Addictive substance theorists assert that our brains are hard-wired to find certain things pleasurable, such as eating and having sex. These are behaviours which we need to engage in to survive as an organism or as a species, and they stimulate the reward pathways in our brains to make sure that we do. But there are many things that stimulate our reward circuitry that are not, in fact, necessary for life – including alcohol, drugs, fatty foods, nicotine and sugar. The pleasure we get from these substances comes from an interaction between the chemistry of the substance and the chemistry of the brain which results in the brain releasing dopamine. And this dopamine-induced experience of pleasure reinforces the desire to repeat the behaviour.

Adherents of this theory would admit that it doesn't follow that any substance that stimulates the reward pathways in the brain will always lead to an addiction, but they do argue that any such substance has the potential to be addictive – we're back to the 'slippery slope'. Why does the addictive substance theory hold such an appeal for anti-alcohol campaigners? Well, for a start it overcomes objections about nanny-statism and interfering with individual choice. Once you can present the consumption of a given substance as a form of chemical enslavement that arises out of its ability to interact with brain chemistry and generate a dopamine hit, then people are transformed from being consumers exercising free will, into vulnerable individuals who are at the mercy of biological processes which they aren't aware of, can't control and which subvert their will.

In relation to alcohol, tolerance, withdrawal and craving are perceived as being properties intrinsic to the substance of ethyl alcohol and its interaction with our brain chemistry; heavy and habitual use is imagined to give the organism no choice but to manifest these symptoms and the process is characterised as a biologically determined inevitability that results from sufficient exposure to the drug. Furthermore, this chemically-driven process of addiction is thought not simply inevitable, but irreversible and independent of individual, cultural or group circumstances. The 'recovering alcoholic' is always going to be just that - 'recovering' - never 'cured', but constantly in danger of 'falling off the wagon'. Lifelong abstinence is therefore seen as the only course of action and the abstaining 'vulnerable individual' must be supported by a variety of 'troubled persons' professionals, or Alcoholics Anonymous, or a combination of the two, if relapse is to be prevented. Thus a simple formulation is arrived at: alcohol causes alcoholism.

Whilst it is obvious that any substance that can intoxicate will, by definition, have a pharmacology, the notion that we can explain an addictive involvement with alcohol wholly or principally in terms of brain chemistry is a biological reductionist proposition that fails to take into account a number of other variables. In 'The Meaning of Addiction' researcher and addiction expert Stanton Peele writes: "The conventional concept of addiction – the one accepted not only by the media and popular audiences, but by researchers whose work does little to support it – derives more from magic than from science. The core of this concept is that an entire set of feelings and behaviors is the unique result of one biological process" *(Stanton Peele, The*

Meaning of Addiction, p. 1).

VESTED INTERESTS

Over the years there have been numerous chemical therapies developed: Antabuse, Naltrexone and Acamprosate (Campral) are the most well-known. Pharmaceutical companies have a huge vested interest in keeping the folk-lore of alcoholism-as-a-disease going. Notwithstanding the trenchant criticism of those who doubt that complex behaviours can be explained by biological reductionism, we nevertheless see pharmaceutical companies with a vested interest in maintaining a busted theory making contentious statements as if they were uncontested scientific truths. As an example, consider this statement from Biotie Therapies: "Alcohol dependence is a brain disease with a high probability of following a progressive course." A brain disease? Is it catching? Well, no....but according to Biotie Therapies: "genetic factors account for an estimated 60% of the risk of developing the disease."

Biotie Therapies has of course developed a treatment for this 'disease'. It is called Selincro, and it is marketed by a drug company called Lundbeck Ltd. Lundbeck paid Biotie Therapies €12 million for the manufacturing and development rights to Selincro and a further upfront payment of €54 million as a sales milestone payment. On their website Biotie Therapies explain: "Selincro is a small molecule opioid receptor modulator that inhibits the reward pathway in the brain that reinforces the desire for alcohol and other addictive substances." So, a 'wonder drug'! Not just a treatment for alcoholism but for "other addictive substances" too. And this efficacy has all been squished into a pill that the alcohol addict can take any time he feels a strong desire to drink – blocking those 'reward pathways' delivers salvation - and in the nick of time!

The use of chemicals that suppress the desire for alcohol, or for that matter, for food is nothing new. But presenting a means by which brain chemistry can be modified to suppress various appetites is not the same thing as a cure, nor does it support a theory of causation. Merely because a particular part of an alcoholic's brain-functioning can be 'inhibited' – suppressed – may well modify that person's behaviour, but it is a very big step indeed to imply that lack of such inhibition is the cause of the problem as opposed to a symptom of it.

Peele suggests that exclusively biological concepts of addiction have failed to pinpoint the mechanism allegedly responsible, and that addictive behaviour is subject to social and cognitive influences, just like any other behaviour. In this formulation alcohol dependence is best understood as a maladaptive adjustment to the drinker's environment. It represents an habitual, dysfunctional style of coping with problems that the individual can modify with changing psychological and social circumstances. Addiction is therefore socially constructed, can be socially de-constructed, and is seen as a characteristic of persons not substances.

THE OPIUM MODEL

In fact the chemical enslavement model of addiction owes much to an historical perception of opiate use in the United States in the late 19th and early 20th century's. Chinese immigrants were stigmatised as 'opium fiends' in order to justify restrictions on Chinese immigration. The model of the opium-den-inhabiting Chinaman, enslaved to the iniquities of a powerful narcotic, became the template for both popular and scientific understanding of other forms of addictive involvement, including alcoholism.

In the United States the image and reputation of opium changed when its use ceased to be the preserve of middle class (and female) Americans using laudanum as a treatment for a variety of ailments, and shifted to mostly male, lower class users who lived in the large cities. The reputational change was further compounded by opium smoking and later heroin injecting by Asian immigrants and other social outcast groups.

In 19th century Britain opiate use also involved tinctures such as laudanum and paregoric, but it was largely used by the working class and as such it aroused official concern, particularly when it was believed to interfere with the work ethic. The parallels with alcohol use are obvious.

So, opium use became socially reconstructed as a social problem that was antithetical to middle-class lifestyles and values when its use spread to the lower classes, and when the purpose of its use changed from medicinal - the relief of suffering; to recreational - the pursuit of pleasure.

WHAT IS MEANT BY 'DISEASE'?

The traditional notion of disease is based on 'germ theory' – the proposition that a bacteria or a virus infects the body and challenges the immune system. If the immune system can't cope we turn to doctors for medicines or other treatments that cure the disease. On the basis of this definition it is hard to see how we can sensibly characterise alcoholism as a disease. But as the 20th century wore on medical science established increasing numbers of definitely recognisable physical conditions, such as typhoid and cholera. The success of medical science in treating these 'disease entities' encouraged the belief that scientific progress encompassed medical intervention in less definable conditions, such as heroin addiction and alcoholism. Thus misconceived notions of scientific progress caused what were previously regarded as social, moral, spiritual or emotional problems to evolve into a concept of addiction that medicalized these problems.

Indeed, the popular conception of heroin (which is synthetic opium derived from the opium poppy) as the classical drug of physical addiction has itself been undermined by extensive research into the heroin use of American GIs in Vietnam. Many young American conscripts developed an addictive involvement with heroin as a coping mechanism for the horrors they witnessed during that most dreadful of military adventures. Upon returning to the United States most of them were able to stop heroin use without any of the feared withdrawal symptoms materialising. Those that weren't tended to be black American's from ghetto environments whose heroin use pre-dated their service in Vietnam (see Robins et al's 1975 research on Vietnam vets; see research by Jaffe and Harris 1973, and Peele 1978).

THE SOCIAL SCIENCE CHALLENGE TO MEDICAL ORTHODOXY
A key proposition of the disease theory of alcoholism, which is accepted both by medical professionals and is implicit to self-help programmes like those offered by AA, is the idea of loss of control. Once addicted, the gamma alcoholic has lost control of his drinking and is chemically enslaved by way of biological mechanisms that are impervious to social or cultural influences.

Social science has challenged this proposition and studies that refute the disease theory of alcoholism have demonstrated that alcoholics' drinking patterns do not all conform to the loss of control model; that techniques aimed at moderating problem drinking behaviour can succeed; that the outcomes for treated and non-treated alcoholic populations do not demonstrate the superiority of 12-step programmes and the like; and cross-ethnic studies have demonstrated that social and belief systems are a major component in alcoholism. In fact, far from being an irreversible condition, many people with an addictive involvement with alcohol do return to controlled drinking, usually when their life circumstances change for the better.

In fact the proposition that addictions are caused wholly or mainly by substances not only fails to explain non-substance addictions, such as gambling, sex or running addictions, but also serves the interests of those involved in the New Public Health Movement (NPHM) in a variety of ways. 'Movement politics' facilitates the submergence of activists with anti-business politics and policies. It disguises their politics and provides their views with a spurious scientific justification.

Additionally, the notion of addictive substances provides the NPHM with a useful tool that assists them in two main ways. Firstly, it is portable. Consider the views of American scientist Robert Lustig, who has led the campaign against the sugar industry, particularly in relation to fizzy drinks. He believes that sugar is "dangerous, addictive and toxic." In a nutrition symposium in March 2013 he said: "This is a war, and you didn't even know you were fighting it" (The Sunday Times, 28/04/13). So the notion of addictive substances has migrated from narcotics like opium, to tobacco, to alcohol and now to sugar.

Anti-sugar campaigners have developed this into a conspiracy theory: Big Food is deliberately addicting its customers by stealth to sugar-saturated products which they will have to buy more of to satisfy their cravings. Oh my! This isn't paranoia, honest! They really are out to get us, so alert the media, alarm the public by relentless risk-inflation and before you know it you've got a full-blown moral panic. Sound familiar?

Secondly, since the notion of addictive substances implies compulsion and a loss of control by the addict, coercive, legislative measures are thereby justified to save 'vulnerable' individuals and groups from 'exploitation' by Big Tobacco, Big Alcohol and Big Sugar. My purpose in making this argument is not to suggest that we should all light-up, drink to get drunk or eat deep-fried Mars Bars, but rather to point out how NPHM activists use misbegotten and refuted science to justify coercive measures in a way that advances their anti-business agenda.

SUBSTANCE, SET AND SETTING

A more useful paradigm is that implied by the title above. Clearly any substance that can change consciousness and provide users with an experience that they want to repeat is part of the picture; but only a part. The 'set' – the mind-set of the user, his or her psychology and life-experience, what has brought the user to the point that he or she values a drug experience is hugely important. The 'setting' – the social environment in which alcohol or other drug use takes place is also instrumental in reinforcing the habitual nature of the behaviour. It is the social environment in which drug use takes place that enables the user to learn what 'getting high' or 'getting merry' means, and to interpret these experiences as being pleasurable. In this construction the substance is simply the object of the addiction, not the cause of it. In relation to alcohol this might be encapsulated by the aphorism "It's the Thinking, not the Drinking." Taken together, substance, set and setting constitute the architecture of a socially constructed addictive involvement.

THE SOCIAL CLASS DIMENSION

The notion that drink causes drinking problems is further debunked by recent research that demonstrates that it's the money in your pocket that determines whether you have a drink problem, not chemical mechanisms. In 2010 the North West Public Health Observatory published a series of reports that break down drinking patterns and alcohol problems into different population segments. The purpose of this research was to facilitate a more accurate targeting of health interventions and social marketing campaigns to reduce alcohol-related harms. These reports confirmed what previous studies have shown: that while alcohol consumption is as great, or even greater among higher income groups, alcohol-related hospital admissions are massively skewed towards the poor.

By using the UK Government's Index of Multiple Deprivation, the reports showed that people living in the poorest fifth of the population are 5.5 times more likely to find themselves in hospital with 'alcohol-specific mental and behavioural disorders' than those living in the richest fifth. People living in the poorest tenth are 7.5 times more likely than those in the richest tenth. People living in social housing are **8.5** times more likely to have an alcohol-related disorder than a 'career professional'; and those classified as 'vulnerable disadvantaged' register 13 times more alcohol-related hospital admissions than 'affluent families.'

If, as Biotie Therapies' scientists apparently believe, alcohol dependence is "a brain disease," why does it disproportionately affect the poor? Are the brains of the affluent constructed differently? Once the social patterns of alcohol misuse and hospitalisation is examined, the view of alcohol dependence and alcohol problems as being biologically driven irrespective of class, culture or affluence becomes impossible to sustain.

DRINKING CULTURES

A good, practical way of defining 'culture', in the context of understanding patterns of alcohol misuse, might read something like this: "culture is what you and me get up to round here." Recognising the parochial nature of drinking cultures is central to the understanding that there isn't one, single 'drinking culture' in a given society. The proposition, for example, that the UK's drinking culture is characterised by 'binge drinking' – a pattern of drinking-to-get-drunk – would suggest that an entire nation's drinking habits are mono-cultural and seriously disordered. In fact binge drinking is a pattern of alcohol misuse most prevalent amongst some sections of young drinkers and their behaviour in the night-time economy of towns and city centres.

Three things have fuelled this particular pattern of drinking: firstly the six-fold increase in the number of young people going on to further education; secondly, the creation of an underclass of people who are, seemingly, permanently excluded from the economic and social benefits of mainstream society; thirdly, the ageing population. Below, I discuss all three of these developments.

[i]   STUDENT DRINKING IN THE UK

In the 1960s approximately 8% of young people secured places at universities. Only about 2% of them were from working class backgrounds. Then, as now, this presented mostly middle class young people with a taste of freedom from parental control which led to an exuberant drinking and drug-taking culture. Today, some 49% of male and 50% of female young people secure a place at a university. Drinking patterns are normative. If there is a six-fold increase in the number of young people being pumped through a pre-existing drinking-to-get-drunk culture then it is hardly surprising that this is perceived by these young people as the normal thing to do, but perceived from the outside by the wider society as a growing problem. But it's not a growing problem that can be attributed to alcohol per se, but should instead be viewed as the consequence of a growing student demographic that has manifested itself for reasons of a political nature.

From the 1980s onwards politicians of all parties saw the electoral advantages of turning a university place in to a middle-class right, and this had a number of consequences for our educational system, as well as for our drinking cultures. 'Dumbing down' and 'grade inflation' have characterised our examination systems for the past 25 years. Advanced-level GCSEs – 'A-levels' – have seen a year-on-year increase in the number of young people attaining high grades and qualifying for university places. To accommodate the increase in the number of undergraduates successive governments have upgraded a number of further education establishments to the status of universities. "Tech colleges on steroids" has been the unkind, but not wholly inaccurate way in which many have come to see these new universities.

But government doesn't simply want an increase in educational opportunities; it wants to see 'outcomes.' So the dumbing-down apparent at A-level stage had to be perpetuated at degree level. The replacement of exam-based degree qualifications with a points-based system based on course-work assessment and assignments enabled a lot of students to attain degrees who would never have been able to do so under the old, exam-based system. The UK has many excellent universities, but, sadly, also has many sub-standard degree factories.

So when government and politicians castigate the licensed retail sector for competing for the student pound, and admonish it to promote responsible drinking amongst the student population and young people generally, they are expecting alcohol sellers to mitigate problems that are the unwitting and unintended consequence of political processes for which they are not responsible.

[ii]   THE UNDERCLASS

The term 'underclass' is attributed to sociologist Gunnar Myrdal, who wrote in the 1960s of the existence of a class of people below the economic level of the traditional working class, who were unemployed and unemployable. In the 1980s the term was popularised by American New Right thinkers like Charles Murray. Considerable debate has focussed on the existence of such a class and about the way in which 'welfarism' contributes to the longevity and inter-generational nature of poverty.

There seems little doubt, however, that young people, and in particular young men who are, to use the current jargon, 'NEETS' – not in employment, education or training – figure significantly in the alcohol-fuelled crime statistics. Thus we see the incongruous phenomenon of an uninhibited middle-class student population interacting with a feral underclass of un-socialised youth in the context of a sybaritic night-time economy. No wonder the traditional middle-class of the shires and the media that articulates their uncomprehending concerns are alarmed!

[iii]   THE AGEING POPULATION

The UK's population is ageing as a result of falling birth rates and increased life-expectancy. For the first time we have more people aged over 55 than aged under 25 years old. This has implications for drinking cultures and drinking problems. Pensioner poverty and social isolation drives problem drinking amongst the elderly and the link between pensions and inflation has only recently been restored.

The social processes that drive drinking problems amongst the young Linked to the problem of student drinking and to the problem of chaotic drinking amongst unemployed young men are two further problems: firstly, the focus on eliminating underage drinking (drinking before the legal age of purchase – 18 years), and secondly, the breakdown of the two-parent nuclear family, particularly amongst the underclass – indeed, this breakdown is seen by some as central to its development.

[i]   UNDERAGE SALES PREVENTION

A minimum age of purchase for alcohol has been enshrined in UK law since 1916. However, the obsessive focus on preventing underage drinking is a relatively recent phenomenon. Only since the advent of the Licensing

Act 2003 have we seen this issue achieve a prominence that it had not previously achieved.

Ask almost anyone of the post-war generation whether they waited until they were 18 years old before buying a drink in a pub or social club and the answer would be "no." Fathers taking their 16 or 17 year-old sons to the pub or the working man's club and buying them a pint is a tradition that goes back generations; groups of young girls flirting their way past the bouncers in nightclubs has likewise been a time-honoured tradition. Landlords turning a 'blind-eye' to a well-behaved 16 or 17 year-old drinker is similarly a well-observed practice.

There is an implicit social compact to such cultural traditions. The landlord, by tolerating a degree of underage drinking was implicitly saying to the young drinker "if you want to take part in an adult ritual then you'd better conduct yourself like one." Similarly, the young drinker was entitled to infer that if he had a couple of drinks and 'behaved himself', then he would be given the informal status of apprentice/adult drinker.

The medical temperance obsession with protecting the young from the evils of alcohol has put an end to the informal rituals whereby young people were socialised into a responsible use of alcohol, and replaced it with an absolute prohibition that raises the mystique and allure of alcohol whilst doing nothing to temper that with any kind of social training. The result is that underage drinkers are denied access to controlled drinking in pubs and clubs and experiment with alcohol stolen from home, or provided by indulgent middle class parents, or proxy-purchased from off-licences and consumed in the park. And then we act surprised when a person turns 18 and doesn't know how to drink in a responsible manner when they enter the night-time economy legitimately for the first time.

The culture of underage sales prevention has been facilitated by a change in the law that allows the police to employ underage young people to take part in test-purchase operations designed to catch-out retailers, most of whom are making the sale by error, not intent. This legalised form of entrapment has destroyed the informal processes of socialisation into the adult world of drinking that inculcated the idea that you should 'know your limits', and only an idiot would not!

[*ii*] THE BREAKDOWN OF THE TWO-PARENT NUCLEAR FAMILY

Over the past 30 years we have seen the breakdown of the two-parent nuclear family as the principal socialising agent of society; Myrdal and Murray both argue that this has been a major contributing factor to the development of the underclass. Single girls who get impregnated by local boys, but then marry the State as the more reliable provider, has led to a huge growth in the number of 'lads without dads' growing-up on sink estates where they are socialised by gang culture, and initiated in the rituals of multiple-drug abuse as well as drinking-to-get-drunk; young men lying around all day smoking skunk and drinking cheap booze, and coming into town at the weekend to violently act out the dramas of their personal relationships and disturbed personalities in a public space, drives what is then characterised as 'alcohol-related' violence and disorder. The alcohol retailing sector becomes a convenient scapegoat for intractable social problems the political class doesn't know how to tackle.

SOCIAL ENGINEERING FOR DUMMIES

The paucity of 'whole population' approaches to alcohol-harm reduction is precisely that it fails to recognise the parochial nature of drinking cultures; does not address the wider demographics that drive problem drinking and does not target problem groups among the elderly or sections of the youth. The reductionist nature of whole-population approaches depends on a crude single distribution model. Price and availability are seen as levers that can be pulled to reduce alcohol consumption across the whole population; and the health and social benefits will then be distributed accordingly across all sections of society and in relation to all alcohol-related problems from health issues, to absenteeism from work, to crime and disorder. The attraction for politicians of such a simplistic approach is obvious: simple solutions to complex problems administered by a political class reared on soundbites. In short: social engineering for dummies.

'PROBLEM DRINKING' AND 'PATHOLOGICAL DRINKING'

The twin paradigms of 'problem drinking' and 'pathological drinking' have obscured the positive meanings and benefits of moderate alcohol use. In 'Alcohol – necessary evil or positive good?' researcher Stanton Peele explains how this approach to alcohol misuse can be counter-productive:

"Historically and internationally, cultural visions of alcohol and its effects vary in terms of how positive or negative they are and the likely consequences that they attach to alcohol consumption. The dominant contemporary vision of alcohol in the United States is that alcohol (a) is primarily negative and has exclusively hazardous consequences, (b) leads frequently to uncontrollable behavior, and (c) is something that young people should be warned against. The consequences of this vision are that when children do drink (which teenagers regularly do), they know of no alternative but excessive, intense consumption patterns, leading them frequently to drink to intoxication."

As Peele goes on to argue, the evidence suggests that moderate alcohol use, when enjoyed as part of an integrated lifestyle, has positive effects – both in terms of subjective health improvements (mood elevation and enjoyment) and in terms of improved physical health and longevity. Even in the United States, the cradle of temperance and prohibition, there is growing recognition of the health benefits of moderate alcohol use. In 2010 the US Department of Agriculture published Dietary Guidelines for Americans. Chapter 3 entitled "Foods and Food Components to Reduce" written by America's leading health researchers states:

"Alcohol consumption may have beneficial effects when consumed in moderation (up to two drinks daily). Strong evidence from observational studies has shown that moderate alcohol consumption is associated with a lower risk of cardiovascular disease. Moderate alcohol consumption also is associated with reduced risk of all-cause mortality among middle-aged and older adults and may help to keep cognitive function intact with age."

The proposition that moderate, daily use of alcohol is associated with living and remaining mentally alert for longer sounds completely counter-intuitive today. This is precisely because the debate about alcohol is so one-sided and we are thereby conditioned only to see alcohol in a negative way.

Likewise we see scientific evidence on the cancer risks of alcohol use evolving. For example, recent epidemiological research conducted in Canada about the risk of developing womb cancer (endometrial cancer) arising out of moderate alcohol use has shown an inverse association between modest lifetime consumption and endometrial cancer (type I or II). As compared with lifetime abstainers, lifetime moderate consumers of all types of alcohol have a reduced lifetime risk of between 35% and 38% (CM Friedenreich; TP Speidel et al Case-control study of lifetime alcohol consumption and endometrial cancer risk. Cancer Causes and Control, Vol 24, No 11, 2013 pp. 1995-2003).

THE POSITIVE SOCIAL MEANINGS OF ALCOHOL USE

Most people drink for enjoyment and are able to self-regulate and drink in moderation. This may appear to be a statement of the obvious, but when stated in the context of the current moral panic over alcohol in the UK, and more particularly in Scotland, it is positively subversive. And drinking standards are normative – people subconsciously absorb the drinking norms of the society around them: "In Italy drinking is seen as an everyday part of social life but also conceived of as giving rise to joyous social opportunities. Drinking in Ireland has traditionally been separate from the family, but has also been integrated into the ritual of special circumstances, like wakes. Studies of drinking sub-cultures in the US have shown that Irish, Slavic and Protestant populations have a high incidence of drinking problems while Jews and Italians have a low incidence. A host of cross-ethnic and cultural studies have shown that social and belief systems are a principal component in alcoholism not imagined chemical enslavements." (Stanton Peele The Meaning of Addiction p.33).

In the US and in Europe drinkers view alcohol use overwhelmingly as a positive experience – one that leads to sociability and aids relaxation. Researchers in the US discovered that 50% of male and 47% of female non-problem drinkers reported that drinking made them feel "happy and cheerful" (Pernanen, 1991 & Cahalan, 1970). National survey data in the US discovered that 43% of adult male drinkers always or usually felt friendly as compared with 8% who felt aggressive and 2% who felt sad (Roizen, 1983, Brodsky & Peele, 1999). It seems almost bizarre to quote statistics that simply confirm what most people do in fact know intuitively: that alcohol would not have become the most widely used intoxicant in the Western world and beyond, or been able to retain that status, unless the overwhelming mass of users valued its effects and its place in their social lives.

The way the medical profession sees drinking – as a pathology – is perhaps not surprising, given their job. But it's only one way of looking at it. Anthropologists and sociologists look at it differently - by trying to understand and explain the part that drinking plays in the way in which people order their lives, separate work from leisure, socialise and relax. And people value alcohol for its aesthetics too; alcohol isn't just a substance that produces different degrees of drunkenness - it has a culture, a history and a tradition of craft in its production, and a variety of tastes and aromas which people can savour and appreciate. All of this is often ignored by policy makers who are in thrall to a New Puritanism intent on pathologising pleasure.

In the current debate about alcohol use in the UK, we see repeated attempts by the public health lobby to include the protection and promotion of public health expressed as a licensing objective in licensing law. In Scotland that is already the case and, at the time of writing, the public health lobby is campaigning for the introduction of such an objective into licensing law in the rest of the UK. But if we are to have a rounded view of alcohol use - one that recognises its positive as well as its negative aspects, if we are going to have a 'protecting and promoting public health' objective, should we not also have an 'ensuring everyone has a fun-time' objective? Most people would instantly recognise that the latter proposition is absurd, but surely not more so than the former?

Part 3

The Architecture of a Modern Moral Panic

—

Chapter 1:

The Temperance Beast Awakes!

In this chapter I examine the recent social and legal history leading up to the implementation of the Licensing Act 2003. I discuss how and why the very unusual step (in the UK) of a radical reform was considered and implemented, and how the presentation of this reform awoke dormant cultural anxieties about alcohol use and society.

I present the evidence that the neo-prohibitionist response to licensing reform represents a media-led moral panic of the first order. I examine how the arguments and assumptions of 19th Century moral temperance have been 'medicalized' and rehearsed in a new form.

THE AVAILABILITY MODEL OF LICENSING

John Stuart Mill argued in his essay On Liberty in 1859: "The limitation in number...of beer and spirit houses, for express purposes of rendering them more difficult to access...not only exposes all to an inconvenience, because there are some by whom the facility would be abused, but is suited only to a state of society in which the labouring classes are treated as children..."

Notwithstanding this early observation of governments tendency to infantilise adult decision-making, successive governments based alcohol regulation on 'availability theory' – the proposition that misuse of alcohol had to be mitigated by restricting its availability.

Availability theory is not really a scientific theory at all. Temperance campaigners believe that it's the availability of alcohol that causes people to drink it. Historically this was expressed as a puritanical religious proposition that had to do with notions of the relationship between temptation and sin. 19th century clerical temperance saw alcohol as the Devil's brew, and those who made it available to others were placing temptation in the path of sinners. Ergo, the more available alcohol was the more people would drink it, and drink it to excess. As any 19th century country parson could attest: the greater the temptation, the greater would be the sum total of sin.

20th century medical temperance simply inherited this proposition and dressed it up in the language of science. But the proposition that availability drives consumption cannot simply be dismissed precisely because it has been such a powerful and long-lasting determinant of alcohol policy; it must be faced. As a religious proposition it makes sense only if you accept the moral precepts upon which it is based. As an economic proposition it is true only in an absolutist sense. If alcohol could be dis-invented, or prohibition of alcohol could actually achieve zero availability, then by definition there could be no alcohol problems. But the idea that in the context of a society in which alcohol-use is endemic, the way to control the problems associated with its misuse is to control or reduce availability simply stands the laws of economics on their head.

The availability of alcohol, or any other product, is facilitated by a retail distribution system. The extent to which that system makes alcohol available is a consequence of the level of demand for the product, not the cause of it. In the UK we have seen an 18.9% fall in alcohol consumption overall since 2004, using the broad definition of population; or a 16.7% fall if you define population as persons aged 15 and older. This hasn't happened because there has been a spontaneous contraction in the size of the retail distribution system. The tobacco smoking ban, the alcohol duty escalator, the economic crisis as well as long-term changes to consumer behaviour, have all contributed to the fall in consumption. As a result we have seen thousands of pubs close and the virtual decimation of the independent off-licence sector. In other words, the distribution system contracted as a result of the fall in demand and consumption, and not the other way round. It cannot be explained in any other way – unless we think that all these publicans and off-licence owners shut up shop spontaneously and just went fishing.

The availability theory has been enshrined in legislation by reference to three key components for the control of alcohol use in the UK:

1. Restricting the categories of person to whom alcohol could legally be made available – a minimum purchase age of 18 years.
2. Restricting the times of the day and days of the week during which alcohol would be made available – 'permitted hours' – the hours, set nationally by Parliament, within which alcohol could be purchased from 'on' and 'off-licence' premises and consumed in on-licensed premises or taken home.
3. Restricting the number of premises from which alcohol could be made available - 'proof of need' - a widespread policy requirement that any application for a new licence to sell alcohol would be granted subject to the satisfaction of a 'proof of need' criterion.

Prior to the introduction of the Licensing Act 2003 the licensed retail sector operated under the Licensing Act 1964, which was based on the three principles set out above, as had most licensing law and regulation for the previous 200 years. It was the apparent rejection of availability theory as the basis for licensing regulation that was the root cause of the controversy that surrounded the introduction of the 2003 Act.

By the 1990s the licensing regime of the 1964 Act was perceived by many as not fit for purpose and clearly in need of modernisation. Throughout the 1980s and 1990s government had adopted an incremental, de-regulatory approach to licensing reform that saw an extension of the termination hour for purchasing alcohol from 10:30 p.m. to 11:00 p.m. on weekdays; the abolition of the mid-afternoon break at first on weekdays, and then on Sundays; the abolition of Sunday closing in Wales (after a referendum), and an informal relaxation of 'proof of need' in many areas, which was made possible because 'proof of need' was not actually a statutory requirement, but a discretionary policy widely adopted by most licensing committees.

So, what occasioned recognition by government of the need for a more radical reform of the licensing system - one that could not be achieved by continuing with a process of incremental de-regulation?

THE LONG ROAD TO CHANGE

Firstly, the nature and complexity of the existing system itself: under the Licensing Act 1964 a licence to sell alcohol for consumption on or off the premises was granted by a committee of magistrates known as Licensing Justices. These committees were comprised of magistrates who may also have sat in the Magistrates' Court to hear general criminal cases, but who specialised in the hearing of applications for alcohol licences and for extensions to permitted hours, and many other related matters.

Licensing Justices were also responsible for granting licences for music, singing and dancing on licensed premises – popularly known as an 'MSD licence'. MSD licences were granted as an administrative matter and were seldom controversial, which is why the power to grant them was taken away from the courts and given to local councils to administer. The rationale for this change was that it would take an administrative burden away from the courts and give it to councils which were much better set-up to engage in such administrative processes. This required a legislative change which came about with the enactment of the Local Government Miscellaneous Provisions Act 1990. This Act replaced the MSD licence with a Public Entertainment Licence (PEL).

From the moment councils took on this responsibility, the licensing of pubs, bars and nightclubs for public entertainment, as a precursor for what was later to happen on a much bigger scale, became politicised and controversial; and much more expensive. An MSD licence that had once cost £5, now cost up to £3,000 for bigger capacity nightclubs. And councillors, who tend anyhow to be meddlers, became much more involved and interested in the kind of entertainment that was being provided locally, and whether this was causing a nuisance to the neighbours. Certainly for late-night premises, which were obliged to provide music and dancing in order to open after midnight, the division of alcohol and entertainment licensing between magistrates and councils created a situation where objectors and the police could get two bites of the same cherry.

And the licensing system for alcohol presided over by magistrates was also outdated, and acted increasingly as an unjustified restraint on trade. For example, a public house was allowed to sell alcohol from 11:00 a.m. to 11:00 p.m. Monday to Saturday and from 12:00 p.m. to 10:30 p.m. on Sundays. To open later than these times a premises had to have one or more extensions granted: a supper hour certificate, that enabled alcohol to be purchased for consumption with food in an area set aside for dining up to 12:00 midnight; an extended hours order – alcohol could be purchased up until 01:00 a.m.; or a special hours certificate, which enabled alcohol to be sold until 02:00 a.m. outside London, but 03:00 a.m. in London, but which was granted subject to the activity of drinking alcohol being 'ancillary' to the provision of music and dancing and the availability of substantial refreshment. Additionally, there were 'restaurant licences', where the provision of alcohol was for diners only.

There are many other examples I could cite of the complexity of the licensing system and its permissions, but the examples given above do, I hope, give an insight into why the public and the trade were growing impatient with what were increasingly seen as outdated and unreasonable restrictions.

THE RISE OF BAR CULTURE
Under the 1964 Act people organised their night out around strict categories of licensing hours and categories of premises; you went to a pub for a drink, but only rarely to eat; you went to a restaurant to eat out; you went to a nightclub if you wanted to drink late and/or dance. Not unreasonably, drinkers began to question why grown-ups were forced to

go home after the pub closed at 11:00 p.m. unless they were prepared to go to a disco, pay an entrance fee and expensive drinks prices and mix with a bunch of kids! And why must dancing be required? This was bound to ensure that late-night premises were frequented by younger drinkers, unless you assumed that there was an audience of frustrated, mature ballroom dancers that no one had noticed or bothered to cater for.

So we began to see the rise of a bar culture in the UK. This development was facilitated by a crisis in the high street. In the late 1980s and early 1990s retailers began to desert the high street for out-of-town shopping developments. High rents and high commercial rates were among the causes. Banks and building societies joined the flight from town and city centres. The licensed retail sector stepped in to the breach. It became a cliché that "Every time a bank closes, a trendy wine bar opens up in the same premises." The size of bank and building society premises, the high ceilings, marble pillars and ornate cornices made them ideal for conversion from temples of mammon into emporiums of leisure.

The rise of a city centre night-time economy stretched the provisions of the 1964 Act to breaking point. Many of these bars provided only a minimal dance floor and a cursory nod in terms of the provision of substantial refreshment – microwave chips and frozen chilli con carne – was seen as sufficient to satisfy, or get round the law. Meanwhile police officers often turned a blind eye to these developments; licensing justices granted new licences for late night premises without the formalities of proof of need; and councillors granted PELs with one eye on the diminishing income from city centre rates. Something had to change.

"THINGS CAN ONLY GET BETTER"

When the Labour Party led by Tony Blair was swept to office in a landslide victory in the general election of 1997, the triumphant arrival of the new Prime Minister at Downing Street to the strains of "Things can only get better" seemed to presage a new era of optimism and reform. A young Prime Minister, in touch with the modern world, socially liberal and switched on to the concerns of a liberal-minded, new middle-class of aspirational professionals, managers and self-employed business people, who wanted greater freedoms and were impatient with the paternalism of the past, provided the backdrop to licensing reform.

'TIME FOR REFORM'

In 2000 the Labour Government published a White Paper entitled Time for Reform: proposals for the modernisation of our licensing laws (Home Office, 2000). The core propositions in this White Paper made it through to a new Licensing Bill, which became the Licensing Act 2003, probably the most far-reaching reform of licensing law in the past 150 years. In many ways this was a very 'Blairite' law. Tony Blair was a new kind of Labour leader. He was not a socialist, but neither was he recognisable as an old-fashioned Tory. He believed in the market economy and was, to that extent, conservative with a small 'c' on economics, but he was also socially liberal. He didn't fit in to the traditional mould of British politicians precisely because of that combination of attitudes. In many ways his politics are much more easily located in the European tradition, rather than the British one. Blair was, and is, quintessentially a centre-right European Christian Democrat.

Whilst an undergraduate at Oxford University Tony Blair was heavily influenced by his tutor Peter Thomson, who introduced him to the philosophy of John MacMurray, a Christian socialist who saw politics as a way of giving practical realisation to Christian values of community and fellowship. This eventually transmuted, in Blair's interpretation, into what became known as 'third-way' politics. The 'third-way' of responsible capitalism was to be located between old-fashioned nationalisation and unconstrained free markets, and this was to be achieved by a new politics that would seek to balance 'rights' with 'responsibilities.' A new balance between rights and opportunities for licensed retailers, and their responsibility and accountability to local communities, and society at large, was what the new reforms described in the White Paper set out to achieve.

When Time for Reform was published in 2000 it was initially given a cautious welcome on both sides of the political divide. The press welcomed it, and even ACPO (Association of Chief Police Officers) did so, at least initially. The New Labour Government of Tony Blair was keen to establish its 'modernising' credentials; this was the era of 'Cool Britannia' and pop stars like Noel Gallagher of Oasis attended receptions at Downing Street. Becoming more 'continental' was seen as chic, sophisticated and modern.

In an historical first Tony Blair even addressed the French Parliament in French, rather than following the time-honoured colonial tradition of speaking to foreigners in English, and then when they didn't understand, shouting at them in English. Part of the justificatory narrative for the proposed changes was that people visiting the UK from Europe were puzzled by our antiquated licensing laws and their outdated restrictions. The inculcation of a continental, café-bar culture was therefore presented as an expression of Britain's maturity and internationalism; a nation more at ease with itself and with alcohol.

The new reforms would confer a number of benefits, it was claimed. Simplification and modernisation; increased freedom as to how we spend our leisure time balanced by greater protection for those who live in the vicinity of licensed premises; a reduction in crime and disorder that would result from staggered closing times – avoiding the traditional scrum for taxis and kebabs that arose at 11:00 p.m. and 02:00 a.m. – the two 'chucking-out' times of the old system.

THE LICENSING ACT 2003

But not everyone was convinced of the benefits of reform. The Licensing Bill based on the White Paper was introduced in the House of Lords in November 2002. It contained 196 clauses and eight schedules, 77 pages of 'Explanatory Notes', a 42 page 'Regulatory Impact Assessment', 22 pages of 'Delegated Powers' and 15 pages of a 'Framework for Guidance.' This Framework was designed to assist local councils, who would take over responsibility for administering the new Act. At the time the Bill was introduced into the Lords the detail of this had not been produced, but when it did eventually appear it consisted of 178 pages, although neither the Lords nor the Commons had the opportunity to study this document or comment on its contents.

But the principal changes of the Licensing Bill were clear enough: the Bill sought to bring together the provision of alcohol, public entertainment and late-night refreshment under one piece of licensing legislation. Responsibility for licensing alcohol sales would pass from licensing justices, sitting in the magistrates' courts, to 'licensing authorities' which meant, in most cases, local authorities. The Bill was based on four principles referred to as the 'licensing objectives.' These were:

1.   The prevention of crime and disorder,
2.   The promotion of public safety,
3.   The prevention of public nuisance, and
4.   The protection of children from harm.

Under the Bill, all the different types of licence and permissions under the 1964 Act would be subsumed under a single, 'premises licence'. The premises licence was therefore to be an authorisation for all forms of 'licensable activity' to be conducted in a premise. Moreover, the Bill separated the licensing of premises from the licensing of persons. A 'personal licence holder' would be responsible for making, or authorising others to make, sales of alcohol.

'Permitted hours' for the sale of alcohol, set nationally by Parliament, would be replaced by local determination. An applicant for a premises licence would apply for the hours he wanted, and if there were no objections from 'responsible authorities' such as the police, or from 'interested parties' – residents or businesses 'in the vicinity' of the premises, then the hours applied for were the hours that would be granted. And finally, 'proof of need' as a policy would cease to have effect. Objections or 'representations' had to be based on one or more of the four licensing objectives. In other words, an objection or representation about an application could not be made on an arbitrary basis, but had to show how the granting of a licence would undermine one or more of the licensing objectives.

Much has happened since the Bill became an Act of Parliament to row back from the radicalism of the original proposals, but what was clear at the time the Bill began its passage through Parliament is that it was a massive repudiation of the 'availability theory' of alcohol-harm reduction. The abolition of the policy requirement for a 'proof of need' for new licences meant, in practice, that market forces would determine the number of premises from which alcohol could be sold. The abolition of permitted hours, determined by Parliament, created the possibility of 24-hour licensing. Despite this, during its passage through Parliament there was little real opposition to the changes proposed. Apart from an amendment in the Lords that exempted traditional folk dancing from being classified as 'regulated entertainment' – the so-called 'Morris dancing exemption' – the Bill survived its passage through Parliament pretty much unscathed and the

Act received Royal Assent on the 10th July 2003.

THE LICENSED TRADE VIEW

In 1552 a proper, statutory system for the licensing of alehouses was introduced for the first time and placed under the control of local justices. Some 450 years later, under the LA 2003, the justices lost this function to the local authorities. Licensing justices had received much criticism over the years for the inconsistency of licensing decisions as between one licensing committee and another. The publication of a licensing justices' Good Practice Guide in 1999 did much to mitigate this problem, but it was published by the Justices' Clerks' Society only after it became apparent that this jurisdiction might be lost, and it was too little, too late.

Writing in the Journal of Social Welfare and Family Law, Professor Roy Light of the Faculty of Law at the University of the West of England, explained how this particular aspect of reform came about:

"Strong pressure from two main sources, the government and the drinks' trade, precipitated this move. Jack Straw, when Home Secretary, made no secret of his desire to abolish the magistracy and there were plans to streamline the criminal courts system (the Auld enquiry, set up in December 1999)."

But the Auld reforms were abandoned and the magistracy has continued, so, as Professor Light pointed out, the only advantage, from the government's point of view, of moving licensing from courts to councils was a transfer of cost from central government to local government.

However, the licensed trade began to have serious misgivings about this particular aspect of the change, despite having been a vociferous critic of the postcode lottery of a licensing system based on 400 court licensing districts, each with its own policy. This fear was compounded when it was realised that around 400 committees of licensing justices would be replaced with 379 council licensing authorities, each of which was obliged to write and publish a licensing policy. Although industry trade bodies, the British Beer and Pub Association and the Association of Licensed Multiple Operators, did later mount several successful legal challenges to a number of policies once the change had gone through, the consensus within the trade prior to the passage in to law of the Licensing Bill was that licensing should remain with the courts.

But it was not to be. The trade was keen to see most of the reforms of the Bill, and larger operators of licensed premises were keen to see the final demise of 'proof of need' policies so that they could expand without their market judgement being second-guessed by a committee of local worthies. The reform was presented to the trade as a once-in-a-generation opportunity to have a fit-for-purpose, modern licensing system that would enable the trade to break free from the shackles of the past and, above all, to see a new mind-set in official attitudes to the trade in alcohol: from regarding alcohol-use as a vice that needed to be controlled, to seeing it as part of a wider hospitality and leisure industry whose customers were, in the main, responsible adults whose controlled approach to drinking should be reflected in a more liberal licensing regime.

So the trade reluctantly accepted the move from courts to councils for fear that otherwise the whole reform would be lost. The extent to which licensing at both national and local level has become politicised, since the advent of the LA 2003, is only partly to do with placing the licensing system in the hands of councillors. No one in the trade foresaw the gathering storm of criticism that the new licensing system, and the repudiation of the availability model of licensing, would give rise to.

THE MORAL PANIC BEGINS
It is a recurring theme of this book that heightened concerns about alcohol take the form of periodic bouts of moral panic. But what is the evidence for this in respect of the Licensing Act 2003?

The stated aims of the LA 2003 were to reduce crime and disorder, reduce alcohol misuse, encourage tourism and assist self-sufficient rural communities (LA 2003 Explanatory Notes, 2003). The change that grabbed the headlines was the liberalisation of opening hours, which created the potential for 24-hour drinking. In practice only a handful of 24-hour licences were granted, mainly to supermarkets, with the majority of pubs, bars and clubs applying to stay open for an extra one or two hours, mostly at weekends. Notwithstanding the fact that the actual change belied the headlines, there was widespread public concern both before and following the implementation of the reform. This concern was stoked by the Labour Government's text message campaign just before the 2001 General Election when young voters were urged: "Don't give a XXXX for last orders? Vote Labour on Thursday." The impression given was one of 'let partying commence.'

It was in the period from the 10th July 2003 to when the new Act went 'live' on the 24th November 2005 that the penny finally dropped as to just how much of a challenge to the traditional way of viewing and regulating alcohol this reform represented. Those opposed to the reform were aided and abetted by the Daily Mail and the Daily Telegraph - the newspapers of the traditional old middle-class – and together with the police they vociferously articulated their opposition. Initially the moral panic over the reforms centred on crime and disorder, and it is only subsequently that the public health lobby became pre-eminent in terms of reactionary opposition to the change. The fear was that '24-hour licensing' would lead to a binge-drinking epidemic, a huge increase in crime and disorder and the overwhelming of hospital A&E departments.

In the middle of all this the responsibility for licensing in government moved from the Home Office to the Department for Culture, Media and Sport (DCMS). The main person responsible at the Home Office for drafting much of the legislation was Andrew Cunningham, a career civil servant who moved from the Home Office to the DCMS to oversee the introduction of the new law. Cunningham, despite starting off with zero knowledge of alcohol licensing, was dubbed "the dark lord of licensing" by those who opposed the reform, in what was becoming an increasingly shrill opposition. The Government was somewhat taken-aback by the level of criticism for a measure which had seemed to command all-party and media support for its guiding principles when it proceeded through Parliament. They responded by redrafting the Guidance and defending the principles of the Act in public.

James Purnell, the Licensing Minister, announced on the 8th June 2005 that: "November the 24th will signal the end of the outdated licensing system which dates back as far as the First World War. It heralds the beginning of a regime which recognises that the vast majority of people should be treated like the adults they are and gives the industry the flexibility it needs to meet the needs of their customers." *(DCMS press release 077/05, Government confirms Licensing Act timetable).*

The introduction of the Licensing Act 2003 re-awoke the slumbering temperance beast and ignited a moral panic of the first order – one that has been constantly stoked by a rejuvenated public health movement which was able to open a 'second front' in addition to their opposition to tobacco smoking.

Politicians, police, magistrates and journalists were particularly vocal in expressing their concerns. Henry Yeoman's Ph.D research in 2009 put it like this:

"The Daily Telegraph reported that the British Transport Police had serious concerns over a likely increase in violence *(Alleyne, 2005)* and The Observer highlighted how many magistrates as well as senior police officers believed the new laws would increase rape and sexual assault *(Townsend & Hinscliff, 2005)*. Shadow Secretary for Culture, Media and Sport, Theresa May, said that 'longer drinking hours will mean more crime and disorder' (Travis *et al*, 2005); Liberal Democrat MP Mark Oaten described the plans as 'madness' *(Plant &Plant, 2006: 100)*; and Charles Harris QC said the Licensing Act was 'close to lunacy' *(Plant & Plant, 2006: 109)*. Much of the backlash centred on the government's aim to create a more open, relaxed and continental drinking culture – a goal seen by many as preposterous. The actor Tony Booth publicly declared that the British drink in 'a more primitive, frightening, Anglo-Saxon way' than our European neighbours *(Plant & Plant, 2006: 108)* - a point corroborated by Charles Harris QC who stated that after drinking British people become 'pugnacious and bellicose' and 'fight at the slightest provocation' *(BBC, 2005)*. The tone of much public discourse surrounding was severe and near-hysterical." *(Henry Yeoman, Revisiting a Moral Panic: Ascetic Protestantism, Attitudes to Alcohol and the Implementation of the Licensing Act 2003).*

So, what was the reality? Both the proponents and the opponents of the LA 2003 over-estimated the impact of this reform. In reality neither their best hopes nor their worst fears were realised. The Act failed to usher-in a new era of continental-style café-bar drinking, but it didn't result in the much-feared binge drinking epidemic either. Neither did it result in the much-anticipated increase in the level of violent crime that was predicted by Theresa May, then Shadow Home Secretary *(Evaluating the Impact of Flexible Trading Hours on Violence. Humphreys, Eisner & Wiebe, University of Cambridge).* In fact violent crime in general, and alcohol-related violent crime specifically have fallen since the introduction of the Act.

Politicians, public and media on both sides of the argument all made the fundamental error of believing that there would be an automatic read-across from changing the way in which we regulated the sale of alcohol, to changing the way in which alcohol was used. In reality this didn't take place.

This over-estimation of the impact of regulatory reform left each side accusing the other of getting it wrong, whilst conveniently forgetting that they didn't get it right. Probably the best opportunity for a radical change in regulation to make a radical change to whatever is being regulated arises when you are regulating something for the first time. But a change, even a radical change to the regulations for selling alcohol, which had been systematically regulated for over 450 years, was never going to fulfil either the best hopes or the worst fears of those who took sides in this debate.

Chapter 2

The Neo-prohibitionist Attack on the Alcohol Industry

—

In this chapter I discuss the intellectual underpinnings of the current neo-prohibitionist attack on the alcohol industry. I examine the roots of the view that alcohol is "no ordinary product" by reference to French research conducted during WWII, and the subsequent links between the World Health Organisation and the Institute for Alcohol Studies.

I discuss how historical moral temperance and modern medical temperance became aligned in the Alcohol Health Alliance, and reasserted their cultural ownership of the alcohol issue.

THE UK CONTEXT

I have discussed how the new mainstream alcohol research science developed from the mid-1930s in the United States, and how the disease theory of alcoholism served to mediate the differences between the Temperance Movement, the scientific community and a public made hostile to science by economic adversity. The discovery of a new disease located inside the brains of sufferers took the focus away from societal remedies and placed it firmly on the individual and what medical doctors could do to remedy the illness the individual alcoholic was suffering from.

In the United Kingdom the disease theory of alcoholism also chimed with the preoccupations of reformers and the challenges of the time. A population made restive by the deprivations of war, and that was questioning the rigid class barriers of British society, found their concerns resonated with the political class across the party political spectrum, albeit for very different reasons.

Even before the end of hostilities the Butler Education Act of 1944 sought to create the basis of modern state education and recognised the importance of educating not just the privileged few, but the underprivileged masses as well. R.A. Butler was a 'one-nation' Tory politician. His preoccupation may well have been with the preservation of private property, and he viewed public provision as the price the propertied classes had to pay. William Beveridge, the 'father' of the Welfare State with its notion of a social safety net, was a Liberal; and Aneurin Bevan, a Labour Party socialist and minister in the 1945 Labour Government of Clememt Attlee, founded the National Health Service (NHS).

Butler, Beveridge and Bevan – these three men between them fashioned the post-war welfare settlement. The challenges of the time were the elimination of ignorance, absolute poverty and disease. The advent of penicillin, which had been discovered in 1928 but wasn't in mass use as a practical antibiotic until the early 1940s, fostered the belief that new 'wonder drugs' combined with mass vaccinations could end the scourge of mass societal diseases like cholera, tuberculosis, measles, mumps, rubella, polio myelitis and diphtheria. But to succeed these new treatments and preventions must be made available to the masses on the basis of need, not ability to pay.

Aneurin Bevan

Sir William Beveridge

R.A. Butler

This approach to solving the public health problems of a mass society was hugely successful. It isn't difficult to see how a new disease of alcoholism would fit into this paradigm of science placed at the disposal of 'the people' in the context of a growing belief that social and medical problems were linked and doctors would affect the cures. The development of Alcoholics Anonymous as a worldwide movement helped to entrench the belief that doctors must be involved in the treatment of alcoholics.

THE ALCOHOL ISSUE AND THE NASCENT PUBLIC-HEALTH MOVEMENT

But the moral reformers of temperance hadn't gone away. They saw the possibilities of using science as the vehicle for temperance aims. By the 1970s the faltering attempts to find a cure, or even an effective mode of treatment, for the disease of alcoholism led to doubts about the very existence of such a disease, at least in the conventional sense that the term is usually understood. A different approach was needed and this led to the development of a new alcohol public health perspective, which was itself part of a much bigger and new public health movement. The old temperance campaign organisations saw, early on, the benefits of attaching themselves to that movement, not least because it shifted the focus away from the individual alcoholic and back to a whole society perspective.

There are three separate strands to these developments that need to be understood: one is the emergence of a rejuvenated temperance movement in the UK that could operate under the guise of harm reduction, not prohibition; the second is the development of a whole-population approach to alcohol harm reduction that began with alcohol scientists in Europe; and the third is the wider context of the development of a coercive, Statist, anti-capitalist public-health movement that saw public health not merely as a field that is devoted to gradual public health improvement, but as a way of governing society and limiting perceived abuses of power. All of these developments had great influence on the World Health Organisation (WHO) and hence on alcohol policies adopted by European governments, which to this day do not appreciate the radical political motivations and aims of a worldwide public health movement that sees public health as a set of principles around which the whole of society should be organised. In the next three sections I want to analyse the three developmental strands referred to above.

TEMPERANCE REJUVENATED: THE INTERNATIONAL ORDER OF GOOD TEMPLARS AND ALCOHOL CONCERN

The International Order of Good Templars (IOGT) was the most zealous of the clutch of anti-alcohol groups that sprang up in the 1850s. IOGT became a global movement and promoted a lifestyle free from alcohol and drugs. Like other temperance groups it began as a movement based on moral suasion, but quickly moved to a position of support for coercive reform. Members were asked to sign a pledge not to drink and to spread the good word to others. By 1891 some eight million people had signed the pledge and IOGT estimated that they had 400,000 activists. But, as we have seen, the UK went down the road of strict licensing control rather than prohibition, and the licensing reforms of WWI, and the divisive failure of prohibition in the US, reduced mass support for temperance and prohibition in both countries and around the world.

IOGT nevertheless remained in existence as a hard-line anti-alcohol sect until the 1970s when its leader, Derek Rutherford, recognising that continuing to campaign for outright prohibition was a lost cause, moved IOGT to an apparently softer line of campaigning to reduce alcohol-related harm. Initially, in the UK, IOGT worked with the National Council on Alcoholism, which later evolved into the anti-alcohol advocacy group Alcohol Concern.

According to journalist Phil Mellows, the two groups parted company in 1982 after a row with the new chairman who said he had no time for "a bunch of Methodist teetotallers." IOGT walked out and Rutherford, along with Andrew McNeill set up the Institute of Alcohol Studies (IAS) as an alcohol research organisation. The IAS established a strong relationship with the WHO and eventually relocated to Sweden; IOGT went on to develop branches all over the world. The IAS is essentially the money-making part of what is now called "IOGT International." It is owned by a charity called Alliance House on whose Board sits IOGT International itself, the Band of Hope, the Temperance League, the Women's Temperance League and an assortment of other temperance organisations that time forgot.

Anti-alcohol advocacy groups, together with a variety of Royal Colleges, have now resolved themselves into an umbrella group named the Alcohol Health Alliance. There are some 28 organisations in this group, all of which support the whole-population approach to alcohol-harm reduction described below.

THE 'WHOLE-POPULATION MODEL': A NEW PARADIGM IS BORN - KETTIL BRUUN, GRIFFITHS EDWARDS AND THOMAS BABOR

The relocation of IOGT International to Sweden was perhaps more than just a fortuitous coincidence. The Nordic countries of Sweden, Finland, Norway and Denmark had long operated government alcohol monopolies with strict controls, and these countries were the epicentre for the development of a new public health approach to the control of alcohol-related harms. One of the key players in this new approach was Finnish historian-turned-social-scientist Kettil Bruun.

Finnish alcohol research owes a lot to Kettil Bruun. He served as the Director of the Social Research Institute of Alcohol Studies in Helsinki from 1955 until 1968 and as Secretary of the Finnish Foundation of Alcohol Studies from 1955 to 1980. He held a professorship for three years at Stockholm University and served in various expert capacities for the WHO, which is headquartered in Switzerland. He was the first social scientist to be awarded the Jellinek Award for scholarly contributions to knowledge of problems related to alcohol. This is ironic in a way: that a man so academically gifted should be awarded a prize given in the name of a man whose academic qualifications were dubious, to say the least, and whose own contribution to alcohol science was minimal and has since been discredited.

Kettil Bruun

By the early 1970s a small group of addiction specialists began to focus on what could be done at the policy level to reduce alcohol addiction and alcohol-related health harms. 'Prevention is Better than Cure' appears to have been their maxim, particularly since a 'cure' for a disease that no-one could quite pin down and define seemed stubbornly beyond reach. These addiction specialists rediscovered a piece of half-forgotten research by a French mathematician named Sully Lederman. His research in wartime Paris purported to demonstrate a causal relationship between a decline in the city's alcohol consumption and a fall in deaths from liver cirrhosis.

The implication - that reducing consumption per head of population would produce measurable benefits in terms of alcohol-related health harms - was given further credence following the publication, in 1973, of fresh research by a team of scientists led by Kettil Bruun. This research came to be known as 'the Purple Book', apparently for no better reason than the colour of the publication's cover. A young British doctor, Griffiths Edwards, who had previously worked *pro bono* with meths drinkers in the 1960s, was a key figure in getting this theory accepted by the WHO and was the lead-author of a book published in 1994 called Alcohol Policy and the Public Good. This publication expanded on Bruun's earlier research. The third publication that built on the Lederman hypothesis was Alcohol, No Ordinary Commodity – Research and Public Policy, published in 2003. The lead-author was Thomas Babor, and this text has since become the WHO's bible on alcohol policy and the basis of the public health lobby's demands worldwide.

The approach developed by these post-Lederman researchers goes by a number of different names: the 'whole-population approach'; the 'total consumption model'; the 'single distribution model' - all refer to the same thing, a relatively simple concept: the total amount of alcohol consumed by a population determines the level of alcohol problems that population will suffer. Ergo, the way to tackle these problems is not at the level of the individual sufferer, but by whole-population policy measures designed to reduce per capita consumption.

These policy measures flow down in a hierarchy: first, affordability - making alcohol more expensive by the use of taxation; second,

Thomas Babor

availability - licensing policies that reduce licensing hours or limit the growth in numbers of licensed premises of all kinds; third, controls on advertising and marketing; fourth - measures that will tackle drink-driving - lowering the limit; fifth - better treatment services; and last of all - alcohol education of the type favoured by the alcohol industry, and concerning which public health activists are uniformly sceptical.

The belief is that the benefits of policy measures which suppress and reduce alcohol consumption per head across the whole population will be distributed across the piste in terms of reducing alcohol-related harms of all kinds – illnesses, accidents, lost productivity, domestic violence – all will be reduced. But, in particular, alcohol-related health-harms will reduce significantly and quickly if whole population consumption levels can be made to fall.

In the UK this approach was championed by epidemiologist Geoffrey Rose (Rose, 1985) who persuaded the UK Government that the way to tackle the drinking problems that arose from excessive alcohol consumption by a minority of heavy drinkers was to restrict consumption across the whole population. Rose's strategy recognised that the pattern of drinking was unevenly distributed - with very heavy drinkers and very light drinkers at either end of the spectrum – but the majority of moderate drinkers in the middle. The basic idea was that instead of concentrating on a few very heavy drinkers we should try to shift the consumption level of the entire population in the direction of more moderate consumption and as a result the number of people drinking to excess would fall as well.

The fallacy of the argument lies in the assumption that everyone's drinking could be shifted in a more or less uniform way. In fact it is perfectly possible to reduce average consumption across the whole population whilst excessive drinkers actually go in the opposite direction and increase their drinking. In a number of countries, particularly the UK and Australia, evidence is emerging of a decoupling of the alleged relationship between population levels of consumption and levels of harm. Alcohol consumption has fallen in both countries whilst alcohol-related harms, particularly in the UK, continue to rise.

The alcohol industry has, of course, rejected the whole-population approach.

Turkeys don't vote for Christmas. As far as the industry is concerned there is a clear understanding that alcohol is an intoxicant that is vulnerable to abuse, but the industry argues that efforts to tackle alcohol-related harms need to be targeted at problem drinkers whose troubled drinking is symptomatic of wider social and psychological issues, and, in some cases, mental health issues too. The whole-population approach, according to this narrative, posits the proposition that 'we all need to drink less', when in fact those who drink too much need to drink less. Millions of people get enormous pleasure from making a controlled use of alcohol and the troubled drinking of the few shouldn't be used to justify restrictions on the drinking choices of the many, who don't have a troubled relationship with alcohol.

It is a recurrent theme of this book that controversy over the 'alcohol issue' mediates wider social anxieties and is frequently the vehicle for totemic, symbolic struggles between interest groups regarding their status as value-givers in a given society. It is in this context that I want to discuss the third strand referred to above: the development of a coercive, Statist public health movement.

THE IDEOLOGY AND POLICY PRESCRIPTIONS OF THE 'NEW PUBLIC HEALTH MOVEMENT'

What I refer to herein as 'the new public health movement' (NPHM) began in the 1960s and early 1970s, when most of the infectious diseases had been either wiped out or significantly reduced in Western countries. The NPHM drew into the field a whole range of new public health experts who tended to challenge traditional medicine using the slogan "limits to medicine." Traditional scientific medicine, concentrating as it does on curing disease, was critically assessed. These new experts had to justify their existence and prove their expertise. They therefore had to create a space for themselves that took an understanding of public health "beyond an understanding of human biology" as it "recognises the importance of those social aspects of health problems which are caused by lifestyles" *(Christopher Tigerstedt, Contemporary Drug Problems, Vol. 26, Summer 1999, pp. 209-235; quotations from researchers Peters and Lupton (1996)).*

Tigerstedt also quotes researchers Ashton and Seymour (1988) as stating that in turning attention to the social, economic and physical environment

"the new public health seeks to avoid the trap of blaming the victim."
Tigerstedt goes on to explain that according to the NPHM narrative "the
dangers are everywhere, and they concern all; they are outside the control
of the individual. This is the environmental, or macro-social level of the
new risk concept that emerges within the new public health movement"
(Gabe, 1995, p3). But the question this narrative begs is this: if, in the new
risk-averse utopia of the public health activist we must, at all costs, avoid
'blaming the victim', which is what those who seek to get people to take
responsibility for their actions are now accused of, who do we blame for
'lifestyle diseases'?

Although the early research efforts of the NPHM were sometimes dubbed
'communistic' or 'socialist' because they counter-posed the 'public good'
to the interests of economic power, Kettil Bruun, despite being one of the
founders of the NPHM, was not a Marxist, and was profoundly suspicious
of state bureaucracy. Rather, Bruun was a classic bourgeois liberal believing
in the possibility of a planned capitalism that could reconcile the profit
motive with the public good if socially-accredited experts were allowed to
constrain vested interests – in this sense he was a sort of Nordic version
of William Beveridge. Bruun was part of a generation of radical Nordic
intellectuals who sought to make science relevant to society by using public
health principles to hold 'Big Business' to account.

The basic proposition is that society is beset by competing interests that can
only be reconciled if we posit the notion of a 'public interest' that trumps all
the other, competing ones. This new 'public interest' would, of course, both
be defined and arbitrated by the socially-accredited experts who posed it
in the first place. This 'new paternalism' is a defining characteristic of the
NPHM, which is blind to the fact that it is not outside the social processes
it seeks to judge, but does itself have a set of interests to promote and
defend.

But if blame for lifestyle illnesses could not be placed with the individual,
but instead resided with the unconstrained application of economic power,
in the context of the alcohol issue that involved the creation of a folk
devil – 'Big Alcohol' – and what could be done to constrain its power in
the name of the 'public good.' Indeed, what we have seen is the creation
by the NPHM of a pantheon of folk devils – Big Tobacco, Big Alcohol and

Big Food – all of which are used to frighten the middle class, because the NPHM recognises that in Western nations it is the middle class that is the agent of social change.

Whilst the NPHM ostensibly focusses on policy measures and on informing the public, Tigerstedt rather gives the game away when he writes, with Orwellian emphasis: "Only too seldom do moral or political assumptions underlying different public health activities become subject to analysis. For example, the linkages between epidemiological evidence (the analytical level) and practical policy (the political level) are rarely spelled out. If this is done, however, *we may end up with a specific discourse that treats public health as a way of governing society rather than as a field devoted to promote gradual health progression*" (*my italics*).

In relation to alcohol policy specifically Tigerstedt points out that the WHO approach spelt out in the Purple Book - Alcohol Control Policies in Public Health Perspectives *(Bruun et al)* - covers aspects of how to govern individuals and populations effectively in contemporary society. 'Public health' is thereby turned into a question of individual life-control and self-control, aided and abetted by appropriate public policy designed to 'nudge' people in the 'right direction.' It is this second aspect of the NPHM that has led to accusations of coercive 'nanny-statism.' Why is this? The answer lies in the fact that the debate about alcohol problems, and the wider debate about other perceived lifestyle illnesses – that result from smoking tobacco, eating the 'wrong foods' etc., still revolves around the same axis: whether to achieve change through an assimilative moral invitation, or through coercive reform.

COERCIVE STATIST REFORM

The NPHM, in terms of its researchers who fashion the bullets, and the conduct of anti-alcohol advocacy groups, like Alcohol Concern, that fire them, leaves us in little doubt that coercive, statist reform is seen as the way forward and the liberalism of Kettil Bruun has become subverted by those whose moral-political viewpoint is coercive and statist in its orientation.

Co-opting the power of the State to provide clean drinking water, sanitation and mass vaccinations in order to improve the health of the public, and co-opting the State to engage in taxation, legislation and regulation designed to regulate the lifestyle of individuals are fundamentally different propositions. Drinking, smoking and eating the 'wrong foods' are not in and of themselves lifestyle diseases; they are patterns of human behaviour that arise out of the exercise of personal choices. Alighting on the elimination of lifestyle diseases, as a way of redefining the relevance of a new public health movement, therefore creates a binary between individual freedom and the role of the State to pursue reasonable public health objectives. This binary needs to be very carefully balanced.

Just as IOGT International turned away from openly advocating alcohol prohibition, recognising that 'harm reduction' was a way of achieving the same aims by stealth; so we see a similar attempt by those who are opposed to market capitalism. The open promotion of the communist alternative to capitalism is in terminal decline following the collapse of Soviet Communism and the fall of the Berlin Wall in 1989. In any event, there was no tradition of Marxism in the Nordic countries from which the NPHM emerged. But more generally we have seen the development of an anti-capitalist, anti-globalisation movement that engages in an incoherent condemnation of both, but proffers no alternative to either, other than a kind of fuzzy, utopian, agrarian communitarianism. But the emergence of the NPHM has enabled the opposition to free-market capitalism to submerge itself into 'movement politics' and advocate a series of policies on health and other issues - the application of which are intended to subvert flexible, free markets by other means.

So, the NPHM is not just a set of views or policies designed to achieve the generally laudable aim of improving public health; rather it is a coherent ideology with highly political aims that seeks to use social engineering to secure the 'public good' against the depredations of capital.

The strategy and tactics of the NPHM have been very successful: to use epidemiological research to frighten the middle class by alerting them to 'new risks' (which, in Tigerstedt's words "are everywhere and affect all"), which are then subjected by various advocacy groups to serial problem-inflation by the selective manipulation of statistics; to create moral panics that generate interest in the mainstream televisual and print media, and thereby to create an alarmed public opinion that cries out for something to be done. This in turn has animated politicians who respond with restrictive policy measures.

The NPHM emerged in the 1970s after a long period in which, both in Europe and the US, the economy was moving from one of primary and secondary production to one more geared to the provision of services. At the same time the development of 'welfarism', which even in the US accounted for 20% of their GDP by the 1970s, has created a plethora of 'troubled persons' professions. Today, in the UK, the public sector as a whole accounts for almost 50% of GDP and the National Health Service employs approximately 360,000 doctors and nurses. This vested interest is the natural constituency of support for a public health movement that wants to elevate public health to a set of organising principles that should govern society.

THE ALCOHOL HEALTH ALLIANCE

The advent of the Licensing Act 2003 breathed new life into the NPHM in the UK, in that it was able to open up a second front against alcohol in addition to its highly successful campaign to increase the regulation and control of tobacco. 'ASH' – Action on Smoking and Health – became the template for a new public health alliance: the Alcohol Health Alliance (AHA), which was formed in November 2007 and whose membership includes

some 28 anti-alcohol groups. It was initiated by the Royal College of Physicians, and its former President Professor Sir Ian Gilmore is the AHA's Chair. Its membership includes all of the Royal Colleges – of Physicians, Psychiatrists, General Practitioners, and Nurses. In addition an assortment of medical groups such as the British Liver Trust and a number of other public health advocacy groups, including the Institute of Alcohol Studies and Alcohol Concern are also members.

Professor Sir Ian Gilmore

The AHA has done what the alcohol industry, thus far, has been unable to do: unite around a basic list of demands for government action to curb alcohol use despite the fact that this disparate array of groups approaches the alcohol issue from very different standpoints. The AHA has united medical temperance with moral temperance.

Public comment to the effect that alcohol has become the 'new tobacco' is not far off the mark. The same tactics and the same skill-sets seem to be engaged: De-normalise the use of alcohol by comparing it to illegal drug use; problem-inflation by the misuse of statistics; isolate the drinks industry from the process of public policy formation and dramatize alcohol problems by creating a false image of the drinking culture with endless references to, and images of binge drinkers in the night-time economy.

Which leads us to the 'Big Lie.'

THE HEALTH LOBBY AND THE TECHNIQUE OF THE BIG LIE

The Big Lie is a propaganda technique. The expression was coined by Adolf Hitler when he dictated his 1925 book *Mein Kampf*, about the use of a lie so "colossal" that no one would believe that someone "could have the impudence to distort the truth so infamously." Goebbels went on to practise the technique in his poisonous narrative of an innocent, besieged Germany striking back at "international Jewry." The phrase was also used in a report prepared during the war by the United States Office of Strategic Services in describing Hitler's psychological profile:

"His primary rules were: never allow the public to cool off; never admit a fault or wrong; never concede that there may be some good in your enemy; never leave room for alternatives; never accept blame; concentrate on one enemy at a time and blame him for everything that goes wrong; people will believe a big lie sooner than a little one; and if you repeat it frequently enough people will sooner or later believe it."

The above description articulates precisely the propaganda techniques used by today's anti-alcohol health lobby campaigners. The constant litany of scare stories and the remorseless anti-alcohol propaganda – "never allow the public to cool off"; demonising the alcohol industry, and denying that its attempts to promote responsible drinking are anything other than self-serving – "never concede that there might be some good in your enemy"; targeting high-strength alcohol and problem drinkers in order to leverage stricter controls on all drinks and all drinkers – "concentrate on one enemy at a time"; exclude the drinks' industry from public policy formation – "never leave room for alternatives"; creating folk devils – 'Big Alcohol' – and rhetorical typologies – the binge drinker, the chronic drinker, the lager lout, the delinquent pre-loader. But above all, the deliberate misuse of statistics to inflate the problem.

There are many examples of lying-by-statistics that can be cited in relation to how the health lobby seek to create a false consciousness about alcohol use in the UK. But the Big Lie used to bolster exaggerated claims about the harms of alcohol is the use of something many might regard as somewhat obscure: 'alcohol-attributable fractions' (AAFs) as a counting methodology for alcohol-related hospital admissions. The NHS does not actually count the number of people admitted to hospital for alcohol-related reasons. Instead it relies on a counting methodology that uses clinical coding practices that attribute pre-determined alcohol-attributable fractions to all hospital admissions in England. This is a complex counting method, and calculated to send a glass eye to sleep, but below I tease out the complexities and analyse how these statistics are compiled and how they are misused.

ALCOHOL-ATTRIBUTABLE FRACTIONS AND PROBLEM-INFLATION
Recording alcohol-related health conditions on all people admitted to hospital is a perfectly reasonable thing to do, but the statistics recorded need to be used for the right reasons. The main purpose of this type of recording should be to give an overview of the incidence of alcohol-related illnesses across the whole population in order to assist in the strategic planning of health resources. But it has been relentlessly misused as a counting methodology for alcohol-related hospital admissions.

CLINICAL CODING PRACTICES AND ALCOHOL-ATTRIBUTABLE FRACTIONS
Public Health England (PHE) and the Department of Health (DoH) make this explanation of clinical coding practices in relation to AAFs:

"Alcohol-attributable fractions: Alcohol causes, or can contribute to the development of, many health conditions. Academics have been able to use high quality research evidence to estimate what proportion of cases of a health condition are alcohol-related. Conditions such as alcoholic liver disease where alcohol is the sole cause are known as *alcohol-specific or wholly alcohol-attributable conditions* and their alcohol-attributable fraction is 1.0 (100 per cent). For other conditions, where alcohol has a proven relationship but it is one of a range of causative factors, an estimate of the contribution alcohol makes is calculated. For example, it is estimated that alcohol plays a causative role in 25-33 per cent of cardiac arrhythmias. These are the *partially alcohol-attributable conditions* and the alcohol-attributable fractions would be 0.25-0.33. Fractions differ slightly for men and women. Some *external cause codes* also have an alcohol-attributable fraction (for example, 27 per cent of assaults are estimated to be alcohol-related and therefore the alcohol-attributable fraction is 0.27)."

BY WAY OF TRANSLATION: A PRACTICAL EXAMPLE

Below is my attempt to translate the above explanation by way of a practical example:

Hospital admissions attributed to alcohol have more than doubled since 2004. The claimed figure of around 1.2 million alcohol-related hospital admissions a year, quoted *ad nauseum* by health activists, is based on scrutiny of *all* the conditions recorded for each patient, not just by counting the primary diagnosis that led to admission. Many patients are admitted to hospital with several medical conditions. A lung cancer patient might also suffer from high blood pressure. Although it is the cancer for which the patient is being treated, high blood pressure will also be recorded on the patient's notes, and 'coded' by clerks. Lung cancer is not an alcohol-related disease, but high blood pressure is a condition listed as 'partly-attributable' to alcohol. So the recording of this admission episode will be apportioned between the primary diagnosis – lung cancer, around 0.7, and the supplementary diagnosis – high blood pressure, around 0.3; the 0.3 is the 'alcohol-attributable fraction' of this particular hospital admission episode. The figure of 1.2 million alcohol-related hospital admission episodes a year is arrived at by adding together all the alcohol-attributable fractions recorded in this way.

This counting method greatly exaggerates the numbers admitted to hospital for alcohol-related reasons. In addition, there is a variation in coding practice over time and between different hospitals, which makes the counting method useless as a means of creating a time-series that would enable valid comparisons to be made.

Furthermore, the introduction of payment by results by the NHS in England, and the publication by health analysts of death rates for individual hospitals has encouraged hospitals to increase the number of codes attached to each patient. If a hospital can show that a patient who died in its care suffered a whole range of conditions on admission, then that death will count for less in the calculation of its Standardised Hospital Mortality Ratio (SHMR). The SHMR records the ratio of *actual to expected deaths*. The more ill patients can be shown to be on admission to hospital, the higher the number of expected deaths, and as a result the ratio of actual deaths to expected ones falls and the hospital will be rewarded financially as a result. So hospitals have a financial incentive to inflate the number of expected deaths by recording a bigger number of health conditions of patients on admission. In other words, whilst hospitals are supposed to improve their SHMRs by reducing the number of actual deaths, many have found it much easier to inflate the number of expected ones. In this way hospitals are using statistical smoke and mirrors to conjure-up an improved performance.

Health analysts have worked out that the average number of codes per patient in the NHS in England rose from just under 3 in April 2005 to almost 4.5 by December 2010, an increase of 50 per cent. If the number of codes is going up, so will the number of 'alcohol-attributable' codes. So 50% of the rise in alcohol-attributable admissions over that period can be accounted for simply by coding-creep. A further 12% can be accounted for by population growth, mostly driven by immigration. So the claims made by the NHS Information Centre that alcohol-related admissions have doubled are worthless.

This is how the coding of hospital admissions functions as a false counting methodology and is the basis of the public health campaigners' claim that 1.2 million hospital admissions a year can be attributed to alcohol-related causes, and that as a result 22,000 alcohol-related deaths a year occur. And these numbers are repeated again and again, so that eventually the public and the politicians have come to accept them as the truth. This is a classic example of the 'Big Lie' – one that is so 'colossal' that no one would believe that someone "could have the impudence to distort the truth so infamously." To suggest that regardless of why you are admitted to hospital, if you have an alcohol-related condition at the time of your admission that must have contributed to it is a Big Lie.

Some further examples of alcohol hospital admission coding practices that help inflate the figures: "If you're caught up in a fire and admitted to the burns department of your local hospital, it will count as 0.38 of an alcohol-related admission, unless you happen to be under 15, in which case it won't count at all; if you drown it counts as 0.34 of an alcohol-related admission, even though most people who drown aren't admitted to hospital; if you are admitted under 'accidental excessive cold' it counts as 0.25 of an admission; 'intentional self-harm' 0.20 of an admission. The point is, these 'alcohol-attributable fractions' apply whether or not there is any evidence you had been drinking before these events befell you" *(Nigel Hawkes, Straight Statistics).*

DECONSTRUCTING THE BIG LIE
To deconstruct the Big Lie we need to take the headline figure of 1.2 million alcohol-related hospital admissions and look at its constituent parts. If we strip out the supplementary diagnoses from the total, and count only primary diagnoses – the illnesses or conditions that lead to people being admitted to hospital in the first place, then the NHS Information Centre statistics on alcohol for England state that alcohol-related hospital admissions arising from primary diagnoses that are *wholly or partly* attributable to alcohol total around 195,000 not 1.2 million, and that alcohol-related mortality is 8,367 not 22,000. If you then strip out the diagnoses of conditions that are *partly-related* to alcohol from the admissions total, and count only those admissions where the primary diagnosis that led to admission was *wholly attributable* to alcohol, then the figure falls further to just over 68,000. So, can we say with certainty that 68,000 people a year are admitted to hospital for a reason wholly attributable to alcohol? Well, no. 'Hospital admission episodes' is not the same thing as 'people admitted to hospital.' And here we come to the phenomenon of 'frequent flyers.'

In December 2013 Andrew Griffiths MP asked the Secretary of State for Health in the Westminster Parliament how many people in England were admitted to hospital once, twice, three times or four times or more for (*i*) a condition directly attributable to alcohol, and (*ii*) another alcohol-related condition in each year since 2008. His reply was that 26% of all alcohol-related hospital admissions are repeat admissions – frequent flyers.

A NEW COUNTING METHODOLOGY

In response to criticisms of AAFs as a counting methodology Public Health England (PHE) and the Department of Health (DoH) have recently revised the counting methodology for alcohol-related hospital admissions, and below is their explanation of the new counting method:

"The new indicator seeks to count only those admissions where the primary code has an alcohol-attributable fraction. Although alcohol-attributable fractions exist for external cause codes (such as 27 per cent of assaults), these cannot be recorded as a primary code so the new indicator also includes admissions where the primary code does not have an alcohol-attributable fraction but where one of the secondary codes is an external cause code with an alcohol-attributable fraction. This represents a narrower measure. Since every admission must have a primary code it is less sensitive to coding practices but also understates the part alcohol plays in the admission."

In simple terms the new counting methodology reduces and restricts the use of AAFs in the coding and recording of alcohol-related hospital admissions. As a result the number of alcohol-related hospital admissions tumbles from 1.2 million a year to 300,000. Taking into account that 26% of these admissions were of people who were admitted once, twice, three, four or more times in a year, the actual number of people generating these 300,000 admissions is around 100,000. Given that 25 million people in England drink alcohol at least once a week, this means that 0.4% of them end-up in hospital as a result. To turn the statistic round: 99.6% of them don't.

In their explanation of AAFs and the new counting methodology PHE and the DoH make this admission:

"The total number of alcohol-related hospital admissions, as described by the indicators, is not a number of actual people or a number of actual admissions but an estimated number of admissions calculated by adding up all of the fractions we have identified." (*My italics*).

But health campaigners have always implicitly presented 'hospital admission episodes' as if they equate to the number of actual people actually admitted to hospital, when in fact, as the above admission proves, they are not the same. What is clear is that AAFs are used by health campaigners as a way in which they can inflate the figures by a factor of 12 in order to fuel a relentless moral panic over alcohol, using the technique of the Big Lie.

ALCOHOL-RELATED DEATHS IN THE UK

The good news is that alcohol-related deaths are now falling in the UK. According to the Office of National Statistics alcohol-related deaths in England and Wales dropped 4.4% in 2012 compared to 2011. The numbers fell from 8,748 to 8,367, to give a rate of 11.8 deaths per 100,000 of the population. The figure equates to around one alcohol-related death per year for each of the UK's 8,500-plus GP practices. This figure is 12.6% down on the peak of 15.5 deaths per 100,000 of the population in 2008, but only 3.3% down on the figure of 12.2 deaths per 100,000 of the population recorded in 2002. The biggest fall was in alcohol-related deaths among men, which at 15.9 per 100,000 of the population were 15.5% down on 2008 and 5.7% down on 2002. In 2012 in England and Wales 597,642 people died from all causes. Alcohol-related deaths at 8,367 accounted for 1.4% of this total. In Scotland, alcohol-related deaths have dropped by 37% for men and 34% for women since 2002.

ALCOHOL CONCERN AND THE MISUSE OF STATISTICS

But official statistics are not the only source of alcohol problem-inflation. Anti-alcohol advocacy group Alcohol Concern is another premier league serial offender in the misuse of statistics stakes. Consider the following examples:

An Alcohol Concern press statement released before 'Dry January' 2013 (one of their annual campaigns designed to get people off the booze) included the following statistics:

"More than four and a half million working days in the UK could be lost to hangovers this January."

This number comes from a six-year-old survey by Prudential Insurance which asked employees whether they ever *went into work* with a hangover. (*My italics*). This begs the question: how could these be "lost working days" if the employees went into work despite their hangovers? They may be miserable working days, but they are not lost working days. Alcohol Concern goes on to state that:

"Around 200,000 people go to work with a hangover every day costing the economy around £6.4 billion each year." If these 200,000 people missed work because they were hung-over then Alcohol Concern might have a point, but how can £6.4 billion be a cost if, notwithstanding their hangovers, they attended work in any event? Does Alcohol Concern claim to know that despite attending work they didn't actually do anything? *(Statistical examples above from 'Statistics are the Real Cause', Phil Mellows. Off-Licence News, March 2013).*

ACADEMICS MISUSE OF STATISTICS

One of the most notorious examples of academic misuse of statistics is the Sheffield Alcohol Pricing Model, produced by academics from Sheffield University.

According to the Sheffield Alcohol Pricing Model one of the biggest economic gains from adopting a minimum unit price for alcohol would result from less people losing their jobs because of alcohol misuse. But someone sacked for misusing alcohol is immediately replaced by someone else. There is only an economic loss if the job goes, not if the employee goes.

No less a figure than Thomas Babor (see section above entitled 'The whole population approach: a new paradigm is born') has justified the use of junk science in the cause of the 'greater good'. Babor accepts that cost-of-alcohol studies like Sheffield's are "not scientifically credible", but that's OK because they serve a higher moral purpose:

"In a democracy, politicians and policymakers often need to be shamed into doing the right thing, and costs to society have the ability to shame, blame and even defame," he says. "It is the simple, single monetary figure that captures public attention more than anything else."

So never mind if it's policy-based evidence rather than evidence-based policy as long as it fools the public and bamboozles the politicians into doing 'the right thing'. *(Examples above from 'The Demon Drink', Phil Mellows, M&C Report, January 2010).*

HEALTH FASCISM?

I have likened the propaganda techniques of anti-alcohol health lobby campaigners to the techniques employed by Hitler and Goebbels. For the avoidance of doubt, I am not saying these campaigners are fascists; merely that their propaganda techniques are strikingly similar to those historically used by fascists. I think these people are sincere, even well-meaning, which is not at all the same thing as saying their conclusions are either honest or accurate.

Those who quote the 1.2 million hospital admissions a year figure, and the statistics derived from it, either know this information is false, but are so wrapped-up in their own self-righteous moral certainties they keep repeating it because they feel that the ends justify the means; or they have repeated the Big Lie so often that they have not only convinced others of its truth, they've convinced themselves. I am left with the thought that a man who lies to others is merely hiding the truth; but a man who lies to himself has forgotten where he's put it.

THE SCOTTISH DIMENSION

Subsequent to the enactment of the Licensing Act 2003 in England and Wales, Scotland passed a similar law: the Licensing (Scotland) Act 2005. It was similar in that it too separated the licensing of persons from the licensing of premises; abolished nationally set licensed hours, except for the off-trade; and was based upon a set of 'licensing objectives.' These objectives are the same as those set for England and Wales except that in Scotland there is an additional licensing objective (actually, the fourth one): "Protecting and improving public health."

The other major differences between the two reforms are the facts that the Scottish Act only licenses the sale of alcohol, and not entertainment or late night refreshment, and the stipulation that a 24-hour alcohol licence should only be granted in "exceptional circumstances." This last provision certainly avoided the reform being labelled the "24-hour drinking Act" as it was in England.

Nowhere in the UK is the ideology of the NPHM more entrenched than in Scotland. This is particularly so in respect of the Scottish National Party (SNP), which is a party that combines an old-labour style socialism with romanticised, historical nationalism, and it has bought into the idea that 'public health' is a set of principles that should be used to hold capitalism to account. It was in Scotland that the idea of imposing a minimum unit price (MUP) for alcohol was first mooted for any part of the UK. When the SNP was a minority administration in Scotland they were unable to pass this into law, but when they achieved an overall majority in the Scottish Parliament in the 2011 general election, the introduction of MUP became a certainty and it was passed into law in June 2012, although it has not yet been enacted, due to legal challenge.

MINIMUM UNIT PRICING

The campaign for MUP has become a totemic struggle for the NPHM, both in Scotland and in England and Wales where the Tory-led Coalition Government decided not to proceed with a similar proposal (as of July 2013). This struggle has seen the NPHM line up against what it labels as 'Big Alcohol', in the shape of the Scotch Whisky Association (SWA), which has spearheaded the industry campaign against MUP. What makes this contest so compelling is precisely the fact that it tests the ability of the NPHM to fulfil its political vision of holding economic power to account by insisting 'public health' must trump a sectional, economic interest no matter how significant, and that government, as the custodian of the 'public interest' must ensure that it does so.

Scotch Whisky, as a product, is hugely significant to the Scottish economy and significant to the wider UK economy as well. It is Scotland's biggest single export (of anything), and the UK's biggest export of any single food and drinks item by value. Scotch whisky generates £3.1 billion in export earnings every year and is sold to over 130 countries world-wide. It also directly employs over 10,000 workers with a total gross income of £464 million. The wider economic footprint of the industry supports around 35,000 jobs and whisky producers' spending with Scottish suppliers increased by 61% between 2000 to 2008, rising to £1.1 billion. The industry contributes £2.7 billion in Gross Value Added (GVA) to Scotland's economy *(The Economic Impact of Scotch Whisky Production in Scotland, Verso Economics).*

Of course, MUP was not directed specifically or solely at Scotch Whisky, but creates a minimum price per unit for all alcohol products sold in Scotland. But Scotch Whisky producers are clearly an interest group with a lot to lose from the introduction of MUP.

MUP is the 'jewel in the crown' of the NPHM in relation to alcohol, and so it is worth considering the arguments for and against in more detail

MUP: THE DEBATE

First of all, a definition and an explanation: minimum unit pricing means that government imposes a minimum price per unit of alcohol for all alcoholic drinks. A 'unit of alcohol' is 8 grams or 10 ml of pure alcohol. All alcoholic drinks contain a mixture of pure alcohol and water. The strength of a drink is measured by its 'ABV' – alcohol by volume. This is a measure of the percentage that alcohol constitutes of the total volume of the drink.

So, if a pint of beer has an ABV of 4%, it means that 4% of the total volume of that pint is alcohol and 96% is water. A 25 ml measure of whisky with 40% ABV means that 40% of that measure of whisky is pure alcohol and 60% water. A 125 ml glass of wine with an ABV of 12% means that 12% of that glass of wine is pure alcohol and 88% water. But ABV doesn't provide an easy-to-understand way of comparing the strength of one alcoholic drink with another, nor does it provide a means for government price regulators to ensure that stronger alcoholic drinks cost the customer more. To do that we need to convert ABV into units; this is calculated in the following way:

Volume of the drink in ml multiplied by the ABV multiplied by 0.01 = units of alcohol

Examples:

1 pint of beer (568 ml) with an ABV of 4% has 2.27 units of alcohol. (568 x 4 x 0.001 = 2.27)
A 25 ml measure of whisky with an ABV of 40% has 1 unit of alcohol (25 x 40

x 0.001 = 1)

A 125 ml glass of wine with an ABV of 12% has 1.5 units of alcohol (125 x 12 x 0.001 = 1.5)

So, what a policy of MUP does is ensure that the more units of alcohol a drink contains, the higher its price will be, regardless of whether the drink is a beer, a wine or a spirit. The idea of calculating units of alcohol ensures that a comparison of strength between one alcoholic drink and another can easily be made, regardless of the volume of the drink. Introducing MUP as a regulation is intended to raise the price of the strongest alcohol and thereby curb the quantity consumed by harmful drinkers, thus reducing the harm done to them and the cost to society and the National Health Service (NHS).

THE ARGUMENTS FOR MUP

The main evidence cited for the effectiveness of MUP is the Sheffield Alcohol Pricing Model (SAPM). This is a piece of research conducted by academics at Sheffield University, based on a specially constructed mathematical model, and it predicts that a 50p minimum unit price would mean that a young binge drinker will drink 0.8 units of alcohol less per week – about one third of a pint of lager or beer over a seven-day period. Or, they'd need to spend all of £1.14 extra per week to maintain their drinking at the same level as before. A harmful drinker, defined as a person drinking over 50 units per week, is predicted to drink one unit less per day or around ½ pint of lager. Or, he'd need to spend about £2.88 per week to maintain his drinking at the same level.

But a MUP would not only affect the alcohol consumption of binge drinkers or harmful drinkers, but also of those who drink moderately as well. Those drinking within the 'low risk' drinking guidelines published by the BMA – 21 units a week for men, and 14 units a week for women – would also benefit. The SAPM predicts that a 50p MUP would cut a moderate drinker's weekly intake by about 3.5% or two-thirds of a unit for men and half a unit for women. These reductions, it is claimed, would slash rates of high blood pressure, diabetes and heart disease.

Dr Robin Purshouse, one of the authors of the SAPM claimed: "When you look at the range of benefits (of MUP), it's not just the illnesses that people would associate most commonly with alcohol and heavy drinking, although these will also go down. In terms of the overall burden, about 20% is for moderate drinkers who make up half the population."

The claims made by the SAPM for the efficacy of MUP were apparently further bolstered by research from the Canadian province of British Columbia published in 2013. This research claimed a 34% fall in alcohol–related deaths between 2002 and 2011 arising from a 10% increase in the price of a 'standard drink' (roughly the equivalent of a price per unit). This research is based on a similar mathematical model to the SAPM and was led by Dr. Tim Stockwell, one of the authors of the SAPM.

This is the evidence that has persuaded the Scottish Government to legislate for MUP, but which the UK Government has declared unconvincing – at least so far.

THE ARGUMENTS AGAINST MUP

The SAPM is the evidence usually cited in support of minimum pricing. And it is no surprise this Report is so widely quoted, because there is no research evidence as such, no historical data of how it has worked elsewhere to support the view that minimum pricing, as envisaged by either the Scottish or UK governments, will deliver the benefits claimed. This is because outside of government alcohol monopolies like Canada, it hasn't been introduced anywhere in the world.

SAPM is not 'evidence'; it is a predictive mathematical model constructed to appraise a policy measure, no more, no less. A prediction of what may happen in the future cannot be evidence of anything. Evidence arises out of empirical, historical research, not predictive models. The reliability of the SAPM's outcomes depends on the plausibility of its assumptions. Assumptions are made about the price-elasticity of demand of alcohol as a whole, not the price-elasticities of categories of alcohol or individual products. Further assumptions are then made concerning the relationship between alcohol consumption per head of population and a wide range of 'alcohol-related' conditions, alcohol-related crime and violence, domestic abuse, days off work, and so on. Only if all these assumptions, and their interconnectedness, are correct would it be possible to say that the

SAPM is a credible model of how a MUP for alcohol would affect levels of consumption and the harms that are presumed to flow from those levels (*The Minimal Evidence for Minimum Pricing, Duffy & Snowdon*).

To many in the licensed retail sector the headline propositions seem about as divorced from reality as it is possible to get. The proposition that a young binge drinker would be deterred from 'bingeing' by the prospect of having to find an extra £1.14 a week is something that only an epidemiologist could believe. Likewise, the notion that a person drinking 50 units a week is going to be deterred by an extra spend of £2.88 is completely counter-intuitive to peoples' experience of drinkers who have developed an addictive involvement with alcohol.

Moreover, the original predictions of the SAPM about the benefits of a MUP, made in 2009, have been significantly revised downwards in 2013 by the researchers themselves. Curiously, this downwards revision did not publicly surface until after the UK Government had announced its intention to introduce a MUP. Here are the figures:

SHEFFIELD MINIMUM PRICING MODEL – Analysis of predicted impacts of 2013 vs 2009 models

Factor	2009 – predicted impact	2013 -predicted impact	Absolute Reduction from 2009 to 2013 model	% Difference
Consumption	4.3%	1.6%	2.7%	63% LESS
Lives saved in year 1	344	123	221	64% LESS
Lives saved by year 10	2,040	624	1,416	69% LESS
Alcohol admissions	66,200	23,700	42,500	64% LESS
Direct health savings year 1	£58.6m	£25.3m	£24.1m	41% LESS
Direct health savings year 10	£1,074m	£417.2m	£656.8m	61% LESS
Total Societal value of harm reduction	£6.6bn	3.4bn	£3.2bn	48% LESS

As can be seen from the table above the downwards revision to the alleged benefits of introducing a MUP for alcohol range from 41% to 64%. This is the 'science' that the health lobby invite us to regard as evidence of the benefits of minimum pricing.

And the Canadian research has also been debunked – again, by the very people that presented it. Stockwell *et al* presented a mathematical model, referred to above, that totally ignored the actual figures for alcohol prices as a whole in British Columbia, which in real terms remained stable between 2002 and 2011, whatever may have happened in relation to the price of a 'standard drink.' This research also ignored the fact that the official alcohol-related mortality figures for British Columbia actually increased most years in the period studied, and in no year fell below the level they were at in 2002.

The conclusion that Stockwell and his co-authors reached was that the price of a standard drink, currently at $1.07, should be raised to $1.40 for the off-trade and $3.00 for the on-trade in order to get alcohol-related deaths trending downwards. But in their previous mathematical model they claimed it was trending downwards! Their second piece of research totally contradicted their first piece. But different audiences were being engaged. In the first piece the audience was worldwide and particularly British; in the second piece it was the Canadian Government, and particularly the provincial government in British Columbia that was targeted. This is the outcome when researchers start with the desired conclusion and then work backwards – a pseudo-science designed to manipulate public and political opinion.

Arguments that compare Canada with the UK in respect of the effects of MUP are ill-conceived for another reason too. Canada operates a government controlled alcohol monopoly. What this means in practice is two things: firstly, the government is the sole importer of alcohol products into Canada; secondly, that alcohol sold in the off-trade can only be purchased from stand-alone liquor stores, and in five of Canada's provinces these stores are government owned and managed. In the other two there are some privately owned liquor stores, but these are prohibited by law from competing with the government owned stores on price.

This means that alcohol policy and alcohol retailing neatly dovetail, because the same agency – government – controls both. But in the UK, where alcohol sales are made from a wide variety of premises, including supermarkets, the proposal is to throw MUP *as a regulation* in to the middle of a free market, not a government controlled monopoly. Here there would be no neat fit between policy and retail.

What might be the effect? If we look at supermarket retailing of alcohol – often identified as the main culprits for so-called pocket-money pricing – the main effect is going to be on own-brand alcohol products, and other cheap alcohol imported from outside the UK. The effect will be to raise the profitability of these items by raising their price. This creates a perverse incentive for supermarkets to put some marketing and promotional spend behind these products in order to create a lifestyle appeal for them – rather than just relying on the fact that they are cheap. This also means giving them more prominent shelf space. The outcome could actually be that the consumption of these products will increase – the opposite of what government intends. This is the kind of mess we could get into when government, which doesn't understand how to influence consumer behaviour, intervenes in a free market populated by players who do.

SYMBOLISM AND CONTROL

Anyone who thinks that MUP is a magic bullet that will end the youthful carnival in city-centres is clearly deluded. But this is really all about symbolism and control. Once government becomes the 'price-giver' for the licensed trade, the image of alcohol as "no ordinary product", and as something dangerous that we all need to be protected from, becomes official policy. The Medical Temperance view of alcohol is in the ascendance. Their view chimes with government - not least because it gives them a health-concern smokescreen behind which they can introduce what is nothing more than a sin tax.

An online BBC News item gave a number of examples of how a minimum price would impact. Inevitably an old Temperance favourite – super-strength cider – made an appearance in the BBC's article: "Bulk-bought strong cider, costing 87p a can and containing four units, would double in price to at least £1.60." Well, what a relief, we can all sleep safely in our beds then! What they neglected to mention is that cheap, strong white cider accounts for one tenth of one percent of pure alcohol consumed in the UK.

THE LEGAL BATTLE OVER MUP

The Scotch Whisky Association (SWA) has challenged the legality of MUP in the courts. The essence of the challenge is that its introduction would conflict with European trade law and act as the equivalent of a quantitative restriction of the importation of cheap alcohol products from other EU states. At the time of writing the Scottish Outer Court of Sessions (one Judge) has ruled that MUP is lawful. This has now been appealed to the Inner Court of Sessions (three Judges) and they have referred the matter to the European Court of Justice (ECJ). This matter will now be resolved in Europe, but it could be up to two years before a decision is handed down.

It is in the ECJ that the challenge to MUP is likely to be most sympathetically considered. The European Commission has already expressed its view – that MUP is unlawful – and the ECJ is the court whose remit is specifically to consider trade disputes between member states.

I don't intend to dwell on the legal issues involved, but rather I seek to highlight the issue of MUP as another example of an interest-group status-conflict the outcome of which will determine whether the trade can hold the line against the attacks made on it, or whether the anti-alcohol forces will prevail. The issue of MUP has become a bit like the argument over same-sex marriage – the symbolic significance of the outcome to both sides is at least as important as the operative significance.

The introduction of minimum pricing would represent the triumph of the politics of prejudice and political expedience over rational, evidence-based public policy making. It would also symbolise the failure of the drinks industry to mount a united challenge to the neo-prohibitionism of the NPHM, or to contest the medico/crime and disorder frame of reference that they have successfully established.

CHEAP ALCOHOL AND RESPONSIBLE RETAILING

The on-trade, and anti-alcohol campaigners, single out supermarkets in respect of the deep discounting of alcohol prices. Price competition is in the very DNA of supermarkets – and in general the consumer has benefitted hugely as a result. But many argue that a rebalancing of licensed retail between the 'on' and 'off-trades' would promote responsible drinking. If very cheap alcohol is seen by regulators as the nexus of the problem, is there a market-based solution that incentivises responsible alcohol retailing, and that doesn't involve government becoming the retail price-setter for the sector? There are three possible approaches that have been suggested and that might be used individually or in combination.

The first is a ban on below-cost selling. The UK Government is already committed to introducing this, but for it to be effective it needs to employ a meaningful definition of 'cost.' Currently that definition is 'alcohol duty plus VAT.' A more realistic and meaningful definition might be 'buying-in price, plus alcohol duty, plus VAT.' How to enforce this could be a problem, but enforcement protocols can be addressed in regulations. What makes a ban on below-cost selling a more palatable alternative to minimum pricing is that selling below cost is an abuse of market power, and the ban would correct this rather than substituting government regulation for market mechanisms. I am not opposed in principle to putting a floor under alcoholic drinks' prices; I am opposed to the State doing so.

Another approach might be for the government to consider the selective re-introduction of a modified form of resale price maintenance for alcohol sold in the off-trade. Resale price maintenance (RPM) is the practice whereby the producer of a product agrees with the retailer of the product that they won't sell it below an agreed floor price. Currently competition law prevents this. Competition law also prevents producers from agreeing floor prices between themselves for categories of products (price fixing), and if this was relaxed in relation to alcohol sold to the off-trade then suppliers could not be played-off against one-another by mass-volume retailers.

An agreed retail floor price would protect the brand values of drinks producers from the damage of ultra-low prices; and if it was lawful to mandate the floor price at which an off-trade retailer could retail the product, then a sensible floor price could be achieved that would protect the margins of both, whilst allowing retailers to charge above the floor price to reflect their promotional spend. Profits could be maintained whilst the volume of sales could be reduced. It's not a perfect solution, but if government mandates a legal framework within which the market can do its job – which is what competition law is there to do – then by altering the balance of power between producers and retailers, we create a mechanism that incentivises higher profits at lower volumes, and reduces ultra-cheap alcohol and pre-loading by narrowing the gap between off-trade and on-trade prices. And above all, from the industry perspective, it keeps government price regulators out of the market.

The third approach, which has been championed by many in the on-trade, is to get behind the current campaign to reduce VAT in on-sales premises. This recognises that the lack of tax parity between pubs and bars, which pay VAT on all sales, and supermarkets, which pay no VAT on uncooked food sales, is the principal reason why supermarkets are able to engage in deep discounting of alcohol prices. A VAT reduction for the on-trade would enable a reduction in on-trade prices and a narrowing of the price gap that is held responsible for pre-loading.

It is unlikely that such suggestions will be supported by the health lobby precisely because they represent private sector solutions to a public health problem. But if the industry is to kick the ball in front of it and ward off draconian government intervention, such as MUP, then it can't simply do nothing.

WHAT IS TO BE DONE?

The response of the licensed retail sector's trade bodies to the challenge

Chapter 3

What is to be done? Towards a Contest of Meanings

—

In this chapter I ask what can a fractious alcohol industry do to counter the relentless attacks of the neo-prohibitionists? I discuss a case study of how another social group has mounted a successful attempt to wrest cultural ownership of an issue from those that have sort to label and demonise them, and what lessons the alcohol industry might learn.

Finally, I examine the prospects for the alcohol industry of mounting a successful contest of meanings, in the context of a risk-averse society where the societal values of 'health and safety' and preventative public health is increasingly infantilising adult decision-making.

of the neo-prohibitionists inside and outside of parliament has been to fight its corner and to engage in detailed and well-informed lobbying. The difficulty they face is that cultural ownership of the alcohol issue is so firmly in the grasp of the health lobby that the industry and its representatives have difficulty in breaking through into mainstream media and engaging the wider public in the debate. The responses of global drinks' producers demonstrate their recognition that the neo-prohibitionism of the NPHM is a serious threat to the legal trade in alcohol, and must be opposed. In this chapter I want to examine what the industry might do to counter the attacks made on it, particularly from the health lobby point of view.

The 'alcohol issue' has not been the only issue around which a symbolic struggle has been waged in recent years. In this next section I want to briefly look at another interest-group status-conflict, and what the interest group in the defensive position has been able to do to rescue, or at least mitigate the harm done to their interests. It may be that lessons can be learnt by the alcohol industry from the experiences of this other interest group.

CASE STUDY: THE HUNTING BAN AND THE LESSONS FOR THE ALCOHOL INDUSTRY

The Hunting Act 2004 was the culmination of many years of agitation against the hunting of wild mammals with dogs (notably foxes and hares). It came into force on the 18th February 2005. There had been numerous previous attempts to ban hunting including two private member's bills introduced in the House of Commons in 1949 (one withdrawn, the other defeated). Twice, in 1969 and in 1975, the Commons voted in favour of banning hare coursing but neither bill made it onto the statute book. There were three further private member's bills – by Kevin McNamara in 1992; by Tony Banks in 1993; and by John McFall in 1995 – all of which failed to become law.

The main groups agitating for a ban were the RSPCA, the League Against Cruel Sports (LACS) and the International Fund for Animal Welfare. Those opposed to a ban, not surprisingly, included all those who engaged in organised hunting with dogs as well as those whose living depended partly or wholly on the hunt. It is not my intention here to reiterate the arguments for or against hunting with dogs, much less to take a position on the issue, but to look at the parallels with the alcohol issue and how the 'defending party' in this particular debate dealt with what was indeed an existential struggle in respect of their right to continue their particular activity.

The anti-hunt lobby knew that their best chance of success would come with the election of the New Labour government in 1997. It was in their manifesto that they would allow a free vote on the issue.

From the outset the anti-hunt lobby seemed on the front foot. Their advocates were articulate and media-savvy. They were brilliant at summing up their opposition to hunting in soundbites that emotionalised the issue and that were perfect for television. They understood how to harness the sentimentality of the British in respect of domestic pets, by presenting wild mammals as furry friends who were being cruelly savaged by specially bred hounds set loose by crusty old reactionaries in red coats, who got some kind of perverted thrill out of killing small animals. Public opinion swung their way.

TALLY-HO!

At the beginning the reaction of the pro-hunting lobby was just about as bad as it gets. Their public spokesmen – and they were mostly men – were almost comically stereotypical; portly, upper class and *nouveau riche* upper middle class gentlemen in hunting gear, foaming at the mouth at the temerity of the anti-hunt brigade in challenging their right to practise their sport and have their fun. These chaps would be filmed gleefully sitting astride a horse with a glass of port in one hand and a riding crop in the other braying loudly about "political correctness gone mad!" You could almost visualise them thrashing a lowly peasant! Their self-presentation played perfectly into the hands of the other side. So two things uniquely British were engaged in the symbolic battle between these two interest groups: the sentimentality of the British towards their pets, and a kind of inverted class prejudice.

It was only later in the struggle that the pro-hunting lobby resolved itself into one organisation: The Countryside Alliance. When it did, things began to change. The Countryside Alliance began to field media spokesmen (often women) who were much more user-friendly and not at all stuffy and who were quickly on hand to rebut arguments and statistics used by the other side. At the same time, they developed their organisation by broadening its appeal. They widened the issue from just opposing a ban on hunting with scent hounds, to defending all field sports - regardless of whether they were under attack, using the 'thin end of the wedge, you'll be next' technique. The question was raised: "a ban on fox hunting today; a ban on coarse fishing tomorrow?"

Then they widened their appeal still further by campaigning on a range of other rural issues such as village post offices, mobile phone coverage, fuel prices and rural services. They managed to present field sports as being part of a complex rural economy and rural ecology that was simply not understood by the 'Townies' who wanted to end centuries of tradition by banning them. As an organisation they therefore became more cohesive and more coherent, displaying the knack of conveying complex ideas in a simple, easy-to-understand manner.

Regardless of whether these arguments hold water, by broadening out the issue beyond rich guys killing furry animals to 'town versus countryside' they began to develop a large constituency of support amongst rural voters. And highlighting the effect on rural jobs of a hunting ban was the key to this because it did, at least in part, deal with the class issue: ordinary people on low to medium incomes would lose their jobs. Whole packs of hounds would have to be put down – so much for the British love of dogs! All this was too little, too late to actually stop the ban, given the big Labour majority in the Commons, but when the Hunting Bill became law it did so with so many exceptions and caveats as to be virtually unenforceable. If they had got their act together earlier, they might actually have defeated it. Instead we ended up with a law which prohibited hunting live mammals with hounds, but which permitted drag hunting and which would not penalise anyone if the hounds went off spontaneously from the drag hunt in pursuit of a real fox!

The anti-fox hunting brigade got what they wanted – a formal, legal ban on hunting. But the Countryside Alliance's late surge ensured that it was a ban that couldn't effectively be enforced; didn't actually stop the hunts from operating; didn't close them down and, in effect, let hunting continue, albeit after a fashion. After an elephantine period of gestation we ended up with that most British of phenomena: a formal ban that didn't work and whose purpose was largely symbolic; in short, a good old-fashioned compromise that satisfied neither side.

Reflecting on all this, a leading Countryside Alliance spokesman, James Barrington, wrote this in a blog published on their website on the 13th August 2013:

"The fact is, while the anti-hunting argument has remained virtually the same since well before the Hunting Act became law, the pro-hunting argument has developed and evolved. Much more is now known and explained about wildlife management, about top (apex) predators, middle-ranking (meso) predators and about the differences between domestic and wild animals and their welfare needs. Much credit should go to organisations such as the Veterinary Association for Wildlife Management in this regard. The Countryside Alliance understands how hunting with hounds plays a crucial and unique role here and puts this information to good use, coupling it with political acumen and hard-hitting literature to produce the case for repeal of the Hunting Act.

Ultimately, a sensible resolution will be reached, but of course it is harder starting from a post-ban position. So it's no surprise that some Labour MPs who voted for a ban are keen to avoid discussing hunting, just as Barry Gardiner, the shadow DEFRA minister did at a recent meeting of the All-Party Parliamentary Game and Wildlife Conservation Group. Basically, he and numerous other politicians probably know they were conned into thinking that a ban on the use of scenting hounds would be good for animal welfare. *It all started decades ago when Labour was targeted as the party to implement a ban on hunting and for a long time there was no opposing voice at any meetings or conferences. Year after year the antis had an open goal. Of course there were those who jumped on the bandwagon and saw a hunt ban as a useful vehicle to attack their class-war enemies and even now it would certainly be a mistake to think that such people have gone away.* (My italics).

Yet one can't help wondering how all this might have been avoided. One thought takes me back to when I worked for the LACS and how a certain hunting advocate called Ian Coghill scared the life out of us when we had to oppose him in any forum. I remember a debate at Aston University in which the audience, which was overwhelmingly anti-hunting, was charmed and entertained by his knowledge, quick-witted humour, all delivered in his dry Brummy accent. Ian is now the Chairman of the Game and Wildlife Conservation Trust, but I can't help wondering where we would all be now if the hunting world at the beginning of the 1980s had had the foresight to put him on a stand at every Labour Party conference.

I suspect we wouldn't be looking down the wrong end of an unprincipled, unworkable and detrimental Hunting Act."

Those of us who have watched the developing war on alcohol should note the bit about "year after year the antis had an open goal." Today the Countryside Alliance is a campaigning organisation to be reckoned with. In 2001 the Economist described them as "The main lobbying group on rural issues." It's worth thinking about how they got to that point: if you find yourself in a position where your sport is condemned by an organisation as mainstream and respectable as the RSPCA, you've really only got two choices. You can say, in effect "Well that's the end of the road, if the RSPCA says fox hunting is cruel who's going to believe us when we say it isn't? We might as well throw in the towel and go fishing!" Or you can say: "Fishing is what they'll go after next – let's make our stand here!"

Whether the Countryside Alliance is right or wrong about the ethics of hunting is not my point. They stood their ground, broadened out the issues and gained public support; they challenged the arguments, statistics and emotionalisation of the other side; they painstakingly began to construct an alternative narrative to the one provided by their opponents. I have referred earlier in this book to what Joseph R. Gusfield calls a "contest of meanings." A contest of meanings is exactly what they have engaged in with the anti-hunt lobby, and that is what has enabled them to mitigate the harms done to their cause by not manning the goal-mouth at the outset of the game.

I don't know whether they'll succeed in repealing the ban on hunting with dogs. Even Tony Blair now says he regrets having supported the ban. But the smugness of the winning side in an interest-group status-conflict like this can often lead to complacency. No doubt those who campaigned so successfully for the prohibition of alcohol in the USA thought the battle was won for all time. Thirteen years later prohibition was repealed. Things have a way of coming around.

It seems to me that the debate about hunting took place between two opposing interest groups both of which were passionate in their moral certainties, but between them it is doubtful that their constituencies of support added up to much more than 5% of the population. In respect of alcohol, the vast majority of the population in this country drink alcohol every week, so the potential for developing a large constituency of support is huge. And this is what has been lacking in the effort of the licensed retail sector in opposing health lobby attacks: a unified response that cuts through to mainstream media and attempts to influence the public opinion on which politicians ride. The demonstrations in 1855 and the 'People's Protest' of 1908 both did that.

More recently, the successful attempt in 2013 to persuade the Tory-led Coalition Government stop the inflation-plus rises in beer duty were the result of a well-argued campaign, but crucially, much of the heavy lifting and the gathering of support for the petition and the lobby of Parliament was done by CAMRA – the Campaign for Real Ale – a large, grass roots organisation.

TOWARDS A CONTEST OF MEANINGS

So, what are the chances that a disparate alcohol industry can mount a successful contest of meanings that engages public opinion, counters the pejorative definition of pleasure that is implicit to the health lobby attack on the industry, and that can engage a wide constituency of support in the general population?

I think the lessons of the hunting ban need to be learnt. Firstly, there is a need to broaden out the issue beyond alcohol and the twin paradigms of problem drinking and chronic drinking. The campaign against alcohol needs to be placed into the context of the NPHM's perspective on lifestyle diseases more generally, and to challenge the view that government policy must be based on epidemiology and the implicit notion that it is possible, or even desirable to eliminate all risk from human existence.

People in advanced Western nations live longer and healthier lives than ever before. And yet there is a widespread conviction that the modern

Western diet, alcohol consumption and general lifestyle are uniquely unhealthy and should be represented as a collection of risk factors that need to be eliminated - in respect of degenerative diseases like cancers, heart disease and stroke. This impression is confirmed by health scares like CJD from cattle, salmonella in eggs, bird flu and countless other examples of fears that we are about to be engulfed in a new age of pandemics.

'NANNY-STATISM'

The NPHM has persuaded governments that people must be protected from these problems and in the process must accept an unprecedented degree of supervision of, and intervention in their personal lives. This is often referred to as 'nanny-statism', and although this term makes public health activists groan and roll their eyes, there is a strong strain of individualism and libertarianism in our society that it is possible to tap into in order to construct a different narrative to the health lobby. If this is done, and if the industry engages in an effective contest of meanings, then it is possible to avoid the long-term damage to industry, investment and jobs arising out of the pursuit of a dystopian public health vision of a risk-free society.

Ever since the New Labour government declared, in 1999, its commitment to the promotion of health and the prevention of lifestyle diseases in the White Paper Saving Lives: Our Healthier Nation (DoH 1999), we have had an unprecedented involvement of government in controlling lifestyles as the key to reducing premature mortality and promoting ever-increasing longevity. There is an almost unquestioning acceptance of the fundamental assumptions of these programmes. It is, for example, taken as self-evident that increasing life expectancy is an aspiration we would all want to support. As a result of this presumption no justification is ever advanced for it. But there is no obvious reason why this should be the ultimate goal of medical science, let alone government policy.

There is scientific debate about whether significant further increases in life expectancy are possible, but almost no one debates whether it is desirable. Probably most people would say that they want to live as long as they can, provided that their quality of life is good and they don't become a burden to others. Can we envisage what it would be like if people live, on average, to a 110 years old? Is it really possible to achieve that quantity of life combined with a good quality of life, and if so, then what? Just drop dead with conveniently little cost to the NHS? And if it is possible, has anyone figured out the consequences for the economy, for work, for pensions and for health costs? Can we really envisage a time when 'healthier lifestyles' will mean that we will work until we are 95, and then enjoy a healthy, fulfilling 15 years of retirement?

It is, in my view, probable that we are getting ever-closer to the biological limit of human longevity. It is surely incongruous that at a time when people in the West enjoy low infant mortality; are not troubled by pestilence and famine; have virtually vanquished the old pandemics that used to kill us off; and are living longer lives than at any time in human history, and yet government appears intent on ever-greater interventions in people's lifestyles to improve health and lengthen life.

Alcohol choices and food choices are increasingly linked. As the licensed retail sector becomes more family-friendly and food-oriented, and the pub is rebranded as a middle class institution, it is right to identify as a threat the demands from the health lobby for ever-more restrictive regulation not just on alcohol, but on food-menu labelling showing fat, sugar, salt and calorie content; banning salt from the table; supersize controls and all-you-can-eat bans. Whilst I understand the common sense of wanting to kick the ball in front of us by portraying the pub, and good pub food, as providing healthy eating options, if we uncritically accept much of the shoddy science surrounding the moral panics over binge drinking epidemics, obesity timebombs and lifestyle diseases, then we will end up in the same position in relation to food that we occupy in relation to alcohol. Conceding that 'we all need to drink less' when in fact we don't, puts us in a position where all we have to offer is a voluntary deal to achieve a false health goal, as the lesser of two evils when compared with coercive legislation like minimum pricing. My point is a contest of meanings involves challenging the definition of the problem, not just the definition of the solution.

EPIDEMIOLOGICAL TRANSITION

The key transition in public and political perception of the next steps forward in public health has been the rise of epidemiology and the identification of risk factors for degenerative disease, together with a corresponding desire to eliminate them. Abdel Omran, an American epidemiologist, first posited the notion of 'epidemiological transition' in 1971. He offered a history of humanity in three ages: 'pestilence and famine' (life expectancy 20 to 40 years); 'receding pandemics' (life expectancy 30 to 50 years); and 'degenerative and man-made diseases' (life expectancy more than 50 years). The 'receding pandemics' of infectious disease receded for three main reasons: sanitation, vaccination and medication (antibiotics). But modern medicine has seemed powerless when dealing with the so-called man-made diseases of cancers, strokes, diabetes and dementia.

As a result the NPHM has seized upon lifestyle regulation as offering a way forward. But does it? Deaths from cancers and heart disease occur overwhelmingly amongst those aged 65 and older. 85% of those who die from coronary heart disease are over 65. These are the diseases of old age. In 1900 very few people were dying of these diseases; but in 1900 average life expectancy at birth was 47 years for men and 50 years for women. According to the UK Department for Work and Pensions a boy born in 2010 has an average life expectancy of 91 years and six months; a girl 94 years. Middle age officially begins at age 47! In 1900, infant mortality was around 16% - 163 out of every 1,000 children born never made it to their first birthday; today infant mortality is just 0.7% - only 7 children out of every 1,000 fail to survive their first year. Put simply, people in the UK weren't dying from cancers and heart disease because they never made it to old age - something else carried them off first.

The NPHM would argue that they're not interested so much in extending average life-expectancy as in preventing premature death. Around 95,000 people a year die before the age of 65; over 35,000 of these deaths are from cancers and 25,000 from heart disease and strokes; and around 6,500 deaths a year are directly attributable to alcohol-related diseases such as alcoholic liver disease. It is argued that many of these deaths could be prevented if people stop smoking, modify their diet, drink sensibly and exercise more. But actually death isn't 'preventable.' We can only postpone it. If we do see a significant increase in average longevity it will, in my view, come about as a result of medical science advances, particularly in relation to the treatment or prevention of cancers and dementia. It is doubtful that changes to lifestyle are going to lead to ever-increasing longevity.

By way of an analogy: Usain Bolt can run 100 metres in 9.58 seconds – achieving a maximum speed of 27 MPH. Maybe someone will come along who will knock a hundredth of a second or a tenth of a second off this record. But no one will ever run 100 metres in 5.58 seconds achieving a top speed of 50 MPH! We are at, or very nearly at, the maximum speed it is possible for a human being to run. Likewise, I believe that the big increases in human longevity are behind us. The scope for substantial postponement of death from the major causes of premature mortality by preventive lifestyle measures is limited. For example, a 10% reduction in the level of serum cholesterol in the general population is estimated to lead to an increase in life expectancy at birth of between 2.5 and 5 months *(Dr Michael Fitzpatrick, The Tyranny of Health)*. But to achieve this by reforming the nation's diet is virtually impossible. The only diet proven to significantly reduce serum cholesterol is a strict, vegan diet. Any takers?

The alternative is to reduce cholesterol by the mass administration of statins and other cholesterol-busting drugs. But this is hugely expensive and this medication is not always well tolerated and has significant side-effects for many patients. In any event the received wisdom that high cholesterol is a major risk factor for heart disease and stroke and can be tackled by dietary change has now been revised. It is now thought that high cholesterol is largely genetically determined, and whilst still being a risk factor is not the most important risk factor for heart disease and stroke. Fat as a 'bad guy' has now been replaced by sugar. And in the process a new folk devil has been created – Big Soda!

The corollary of the view that trying to modify people's lifestyles is unlikely to deliver increased average life expectancy is to recognise that the biggest threat to existing levels of longevity comes from the over-prescription of antibiotics to humans and the mass administration of antibiotics to healthy farm animals. This is leading to the development of antibiotic-resistant strains of infections, and therefore threatens the effectiveness of the 'wonder drugs' that have done so much to eradicate the mass-society pandemics of the past. If this problem is not addressed then the public health consequences will be catastrophic. Focussing on modifying peoples' lifestyles in the context of such a prospect seems like fiddling whilst Rome burns.

The issues of drinking, diet and health are by no means as scientifically settled as people are often led to believe. So I think that with food, just as with alcohol, we have to very carefully examine the science and evolve a different narrative. And this narrative should inform our discussions with government – particularly now that the health lobby has refused to participate in the Government's voluntary alcohol industry responsibility deal.

On a practical level the trade and its representative bodies can indeed get political mileage out of the fact that the pub is the home of social drinking, and that food-led pubs are at the forefront of providing dietary information to consumers, and producing cutting-edge dining concepts that embody the desire for fresh, local produce with a short, verifiable progeny. But let's not concede too much ground in relation to the politics of food or of drink. There's a difference between playing the ball in front of us and appeasing public health dogmatists for whom no concession will ever be enough.

IN CONCLUSION

So, the industry needs to place the defence of the licensed retail sector and of the continuation of a licensed, legal market for alcohol, into the context of the wider debate about the relationship between the state and the individual and the goals of public health policy. As I've indicated earlier in this book, we have also to point out to government that the NPHM is a repository for frustrated, cause-oriented activists who have submerged themselves into movement politics because the old ideological certainties of the Cold War have evaporated.

I have written this book in order to ignite the debate; to demystify some of the myths surrounding alcohol use, health, and lifestyle diseases; unmask the pseudo-science that has dogged the alcohol debate, and encourage the contest of meanings that I believe is so vitally necessary if the industry that I have worked in for most of my life is to have a prosperous future.

I have also written it because I believe passionately in the freedom of individuals to choose for themselves the compromises and trade-offs they make in relation to lifestyle and longevity. I don't want Government to abdicate all responsibility for public health, but neither do I want to see the tick and tock of lifestyle choices determined by people imbued with an unassailable air of self-righteousness seeking to create a new paternalism. As with most things in life we have to establish a balance. And I don't think

I am alone in believing that the balance has moved too far in the direction of those who seek to reach into the pub, the restaurant, the takeaway, the supermarket, the car and the living room, to determine these choices for us in their unshakeable belief that they know better than we do what is in our own best interests.

Paul Chase was born in 1949 in Ruislip, Middlesex, but moved with his family to Liverpool in 1958. He was educated at Ellergreen High School, Liverpool and at the University of Bradford, West Yorkshire.

Paul spent 23 years operating a number of late-night licensed premises on both sides of the River Mersey, including the iconic Chelsea Reach which was the North of England's first pub-disco and the venue for Paul McArtney's 1973 TV comeback with his new band, Wings. Paul and his business partner Daniel Davies started CPL Training in 1991, whilst both of them were still running licensed premises. Today the company is the largest provider of training to the UK's licensed retail sector and Daniel is its chief executive and Paul a director and head of compliance training. Paul has developed eight qualifications for licensed retail, and working with awarding bodies has taken them through to accreditation in UK national qualification frameworks.

Paul is widely acknowledged as a leading expert and commentator on licensing law and alcohol policy and regularly speaks and writes on these issues.